YORK NOTES

D0230952

BRAVE NEW WORLD

ALDOUS HUXLEY

NOTES BY MICHAEL SHERBORNE

 Longman

York Press

The Publishers would like to thank Mrs Laura Huxley and Chatto & Windus
for their kind permission to reproduce extracts from *Brave New World* by
Aldous Huxley

The right of Michael Sherborne to be identified as Author
of this Work has been asserted by him in accordance with the
Copyright, Designs and Patents Act 1988

YORK PRESS
322 Old Brompton Road, London SW5 9JH

PEARSON EDUCATION LIMITED
Edinburgh Gate, Harlow,
Essex CM20 2JE, United Kingdom
Associated companies, branches and representatives throughout the world

First published 2000
This new and fully revised edition first published 2005

10 9 8 7 6 5 4 3 2 1

ISBN 1–405–80171–9

Typeset by Land & Unwin (Data Sciences), Bugbrooke, Northamptonshire
Produced by Pearson Education Asia Limited, Hong Kong

CONTENTS

PART FOUR
CRITICAL HISTORY

PART FIVE
BACKGROUND

PART ONE

INTRODUCTION

HOW TO STUDY A NOVEL

Studying a novel on your own requires self-discipline and a carefully thought-out work plan in order to be effective.

- You will need to read the novel more than once. Start by reading it quickly for pleasure, then read it slowly and thoroughly.
- On your second reading make detailed notes on the plot, characters and themes of the novel. Further readings will generate new ideas and help you to memorise the details of the story.
- Some of the characters will develop as the plot unfolds. How do your responses towards them change during the course of the novel?
- Think about how the novel is narrated. From whose point of view are events described?
- A novel may or may not present events chronologically: the time-scheme may be a key to its structure and organisation.
- What part do the settings play in the novel?
- Are words, images or incidents repeated so as to give the work a pattern? Do such patterns help you to understand the novel's themes?
- Identify what styles of language are used in the novel.
- What is the effect of the novel's ending? Is the action completed and closed, or left incomplete and open?
- Does the novel present a moral and just world?
- Cite exact sources for all quotations, whether from the text itself or from critical commentaries. Wherever possible find your own examples from the novel to back up your opinions.
- Always express your ideas in your own words.

These York Notes offer an introduction to *Brave New World* and cannot substitute for close reading of the text and the study of secondary sources.

CHECK THE BOOK

Michael McKeon's *Theory of the Novel: A Historical Approach* (2000) is an excellent introduction to the history of the novel.

READING *BRAVE NEW WORLD*

Brave New World is a **dystopia**: a portrait of an imaginary society which **satirises** the customs of its own day and sounds a warning about possible future developments. Many such books have been produced, but few have had sufficient literary quality or sociological insight to outlive their first topicality. *Brave New World* is a major exception. Although it originally appeared in 1932, two surveys in 1999 showed it to be still among the ten most popular classics in Britain.

 CHECK THE BOOK

George Orwell's *Nineteen Eighty-Four* (1949) is the only dystopia which may be better known than *Brave New World*. There is a detailed account of it in the York Notes Advanced guide to *Nineteen Eighty-Four*.

Teachers and critics often pair *Brave New World* with *Nineteen Eighty-Four* by George Orwell, another remarkable **science fiction** dystopia, which was first published in 1949. The two books certainly have many features in common. Both are set in an England of the future and both describe unsuccessful attempts by a handful of individuals to rebel against a government which has imposed a uniform, repressive way of life on its citizens, reinforced through constant propaganda, communal rituals, state regulation of sexual behaviour and the rewriting of history.

In other respects, however, these two visions of the future could not be more different. *Nineteen Eighty-Four* brilliantly formulates the methods of social control common to Fascism and Communism. Its indignant satire will always be relevant so long as any regime or institution is controlled by a single party which bullies and lies to its victims until they are forced to accept its version of reality. *Brave New World* offers a contrasting model of centralised social control, one which is based not on terror but on pleasure.

The World Controllers' methods of repression are considerably subtler than Big Brother's. The citizens of the World State, from their artificial conception onwards, are manipulated into believing themselves to be happy and fulfilled and are unable to imagine a goal beyond their personal well-being. For any of them to pursue political change, scientific knowledge or artistic achievement is unthinkable; not to behave like everyone else in the social group to which they belong, next to impossible. All aspects of human existence, even the most intimate, are efficiently catered for by a kind of state capitalism which recognises no distinction between the needs of individuals and the needs of commerce. Individual initiative and awareness have been sacrificed to the mass consumption of goods. The family is dead, taking with it personal loyalties, and so too are all the religions which demanded integrity and self-sacrifice from their followers. The great conflicts of the past have been lost in a superficial, postmodern synthesis which indiscriminately honours such rivals as Henry Ford and Karl Marx, Ivan Pavlov and Sigmund Freud. While everyone believes that history has ended, liberating them into a new order free from superstition and unpleasantness, the reality is that they are now free only to consume the material goods, sporting activities, escapist films and mind-numbing drugs which their Controllers measure out to them.

It is not difficult to argue for the continuing relevance of this satirical vision. New developments in genetic science, and the continued rise in global influence of a multinational, English-speaking culture, which construes technological innovation and sexual freedom chiefly as business opportunities, give modern civilisation a disturbing resemblance to Huxley's vision. Yet if we attempt to find a straightforward 'message' in the book which we can extract and apply to our world, we may be disappointed. For example, in attacking the crude materialism of the World State, then suggesting the importance of spiritual awareness, Huxley might seem to be taking a similar view to those religious activists today who attack secular 'Western' consumerism. However, one of the future institutions used to deprive people of authentic experience in *Brave New World* is none other than a religion, the religion of the 'Greater Being'. One possible implication of this is that Church leaders are the very kind of people likely to prevent the pursuit of genuine spiritual experience, by substituting ready-made religious formulas for personal development.

Brave New World is not, then, a text which is easily assimilated to existing points of view, but a restless, probing book. Rather than face up to the awkward questions it asks, some people have

CONTEXT

Postmodernism is a term referring to characteristic aspects of present-day culture. This is said to be less absolute and hierarchical than was the case in the past, for example we have become more sceptical of big explanatory frameworks or 'metanarratives' like religion, science, history and politics; our awareness is more strongly shaped by the media and advertising; we mix high and popular art more freely; artists often leave their works open in some way or produce several alternative versions. People sceptical of postmodernism retort that the idea is itself a metanarrative and is made up of one-sided generalisations.

preferred to read it in ways which simplify its ideas and downplay its continuing relevance, dismissing it as a piece of writing which is essentially backward looking. It is not unusual, for example, to be told that *Brave New World* is an attack on science and its impact on human existence. However, the Controller for Western Europe states clearly that for the brave new world 'science is a public danger' and that the genuine pursuit of science would make the World State's rigid social order impossible. John the Savage is sometimes taken to be a spokesman for Huxley's own views, championing the natural life of the Reservation against the artificial life of the World State. In fact, as Huxley himself points out in his Foreword, the Reservation is at least as repulsive a society as the World State, and it is a society which rejects and persecutes John, not one which he represents. In any case, if John was really intended to be the book's hero, would Huxley have made him so immature and self-destructive? John's frequent quotations from Shakespeare are generally thought to represent a cultural standard against which the debased world of the future may be judged, yet his use of the quotations is sometimes smugly unperceptive and Shakespeare's characters turn out to be such poor role models for him that, in imitating them, he becomes violently unhinged. John's defiant cry that he demands the right to be unhappy has been held up as the book's key affirmation, but in the following chapter when John does become seriously unhappy he is unable to cope with his feelings, with plainly **tragic** consequences.

The problem is not that the view of *Brave New World* as a reactionary **parable** is a wholly wrong one, but that it is simplistic. Huxley certainly incorporates some of his own prejudices into the book (how could he do anything else?), but it is clear throughout that he is trying to challenge himself and us, demanding we think through our notions of how to identify and respond to good and evil in a world where customs are constantly changing and what seems bad in one generation can seem good in another.

When a situation in the book seems to call for a straightforward response, Huxley frequently chooses to knock us off balance with a sudden shift of perspective. The death of Linda should be a tragic moment, yet it is presented comically. The way the citizens of the

World State take drugs and engage in promiscuous sex should presumably repel us, yet they are depicted as enjoying themselves and many readers seem to have felt envious of them. Reading such scenes, we may wonder exactly how we are supposed to react, as there is no obvious authorial position with which to identify. The book's shocking conclusion, in particular, leaves us alarmingly short of guidance. In the Foreword to *Brave New World* which Huxley added fourteen years later, when he wanted to put forward a more positive agenda, he recognised and regretted this negativity – he later wrote a **utopian** corrective, *Island* – but arguably it is precisely its subversive quality which keeps *Brave New World* so fresh and challenging.

In addition to its resistance to pat conclusions, the book has two other major strengths. One is the quality of Huxley's writing. Almost every sentence is stimulating, adding a new twist, shifting our point of view, **parodying** the language of science, journalism or entertainment. Above all, however, there is the sheer intelligence behind the book. Huxley was correct to predict that the development of science would not just lead to new technology, but would continue to alter our ideas about human nature, revolutionise our behaviour and eventually enable us to redesign ourselves – and that such developments would be bound to raise many difficult questions.

If people enjoy taking recreational drugs, is there any reason why these should not be legalised and made part of normal behaviour? If techniques like genetic modification and cloning can be used on other living things, why should they not be applied to human beings? Is it right that new methods of contraception and new theories of psychology should alter our traditional moral codes? Are right and wrong themselves flexible notions which are bound to change over time, or is there some persistent core to human nature and morality to which we can anchor ourselves? Huxley's book puts these kinds of questions in a way which is simultaneously memorable, entertaining and disturbing. Three quarters of a century after it was first published, *Brave New World* remains essential reading for any educated person.

? QUESTION

How successful is Huxley in dealing with scientific issues? Does he manage to integrate them into the story? Do you find his treatment of them sufficiently informative, entertaining and thought-provoking?

PART TWO

THE TEXT

 CHECK THE NET

You can search the whole text of *Brave New World* for key words at **http:// www.online-literature.com**

NOTE ON THE TEXT

Brave New World was first published by Chatto & Windus, London, in 1932. The Foreword was written in 1946, and added to the book in 1950 when it appeared in a collected edition.

The HarperCollins Modern Classic edition of 1994, with an introduction by David Bradshaw, is a widely available paperback edition in Britain and it is from this that all quotations in the present study are taken. The Longman Study Texts edition of 1983, edited by Mark Spencer Ellis, has particularly valuable annotation but is no longer in print. There is a more recent annotated version, edited by Robert Southwick, in the Longman Literature series, first published in 1991 and reprinted numerous times.

All editions have errors in Chapter 6, section 3, where the Warden is referred to as the 'Director', and early in Chapter 17, when Mond is said to have 'exclaimed' the meaning of the word 'cardinal', not 'explained' it. In the Modern Classic edition there is a bracket missing after 'barriers' (p. 39).

SYNOPSIS

Five hundred years in the future, human babies no longer develop inside their mothers but are mass-produced in factories to fit the requirements of society. The Director of the London Hatchery and Conditioning Centre is showing the process to his new students, demonstrating to them how the babies' feelings are trained by conditioning and sleep-indoctrination so that they will grow up with the attitudes required by the World State. The group is joined by the Resident Controller for Western Europe, Mustapha Mond, who explains to the students why and how such a highly regulated society was developed. During the tour, the Director is assisted by another official, Henry Foster, and they meet a nurse called Lenina Crowne, who is one of Henry's lovers.

Lenina's friend Fanny disapproves of her long-term relationship with Henry, which goes against the modern custom of promiscuity. In response, Lenina befriends Bernard Marx, a colleague whose stunted appearance and dislike of the society in which he lives causes some people to regard him as abnormal. The pair go on holiday together to a 'savage' Reservation in New Mexico, where they are surprised to meet an English-speaking, Shakespeare-quoting savage called John. He takes them to meet his mother, Linda, who had been taken there by the Director a quarter of a century previously and left behind in an accident. The Director had been planning to dismiss Bernard publicly from his post upon his return, but in the event he is himself humiliated when Bernard produces his former lover and biological child.

As John the 'Savage' explores modern civilisation, he is repelled by what he sees. Lenina takes him to watch a pornographic film which transmits the sense of touch, assuming that it will arouse him; she is disappointed when he does not stay the night with her. In fact John is so disgusted by the world in which he finds himself that he refuses to attend a party Bernard is holding in his honour. The distinguished guests depart in a hostile mood, shattering Bernard's temporary self-confidence. Bernard turns for comfort to his friend Helmholtz Watson, a propaganda writer who has also come to question the values of society. Helmholtz has been attempting to write poetry and is impressed when John reads him Shakespeare.

Lenina calls on John and tries to make love to him but, although he is strongly attracted to her, he is disgusted by her behaviour and reacts with violence. He then receives a telephone message that his mother Linda is dying and hurries off to see her. He is distraught at her deathbed. No one can understand his grief as no one else has such a close bond to another human being. The children brought to the scene for 'death conditioning' have no sympathy, and even Linda whispers only of her former lover Popé when John speaks to her. **Ironically**, the furious shaking of her with which he responds seems to hasten her death.

CHECK THE FILM
Michael R. Joyce's 1998 film adaptation of *Brave New World* makes some drastic changes to the story. Why do you think these changes were made? Which of them do you think make the story less satisfactory and which if any might be considered improvements?

Distressed, John tries to free the Hospital's menial workers from their social conditioning by preventing the distribution to them of the tranquillising drug *soma*. Helmholtz and Bernard try to rescue him from the consequent riot. All three are saved when the police arrive and pacify the mob. The three captives are taken to the Controller, who reiterates the importance of social stability. This can be achieved only if society is organised as it is in the World State, even if the limits which this imposes on individual development include abolishing the pursuit of serious art and science. Bernard and Helmholtz are banished to remote islands. When Helmholtz and Bernard have gone, John and the Controller discuss God. Mond thinks that God may exist, but argues that, even if He does, society no longer has need of Him. John protests that he does not want to live by the rules of such a society. He would rather have God, freedom and poetry, even if the cost is insecurity and pain.

John finally withdraws from the world and lives in an old air-lighthouse, trying to become holy. His practice of whipping himself as a punishment for his sins attracts press attention. At first he drives the reporters away, but a documentary film about him, made using long-distance cameras, draws a crowd of spectators, including Lenina and Henry. In an outburst of anger and frustration, John goes berserk and beats Lenina, triggering an orgy of sex and violence. Afterwards, when he comes round and realises what he has done, John hangs himself.

> **CONTEXT**
>
> Huxley began writing *Brave New World* in April 1931, and finished it in late August; it was published in England in February 1932.

DETAILED SUMMARIES

EPIGRAPH

The **epigraph** is taken from *Freedom and the Spirit* (1927), a book by the exiled Russian religious thinker Nicolas Berdyaev (1874–1948), first published in Paris. It may be translated as follows:

> Utopias appear to be a good deal more feasible than was previously believed. And we are now confronted by a new and alarming question: how can we avoid their permanent

construction? ... Utopias are feasible. Life is moving towards utopias. And perhaps a new age is beginning, an age when intellectuals and the cultured class will dream of ways of avoiding utopias and of returning to a non-utopian society, less 'perfect' and more free.

FOREWORD

In the Foreword Huxley looks back at his book with fourteen years' hindsight. He regrets that *Brave New World* depicts two 'insane' societies, the World State and the Reservation, without offering a positive alternative to set against them – a deficiency which he was to remedy in 1962 with his **utopian** novel *Island*. Writing the Foreword in 1946, immediately after the Second World War – at a time when he and many others were demoralised by news of the first atomic bombs and by the Soviet takeover of Eastern Europe – he predicts that the immediate future of mankind will be a bleak one, with closed, totalitarian societies increasingly using science to control not only the behaviour but even the feelings of their citizens, a similar view to the one taken around the same time by George Orwell in *Nineteen Eighty-Four* (1949). Huxley, however, sees this repressive society as a first step towards the very different, but still deeply inhuman, society of *Brave New World*.

QUESTION

Compare and contrast Huxley's aims and methods in creating his **dystopian** society with those employed by George Orwell (1903–1950) in *Nineteen Eighty-Four* (1949).

GLOSSARY

ii   *Penitente* a member of a religious cult who punishes himself for his sins with a whip

Pyrrhonic totally sceptical

aesthete one who believes that a work of art exists in its own right, not to make any positive moral or political point

Pantheon a temple dedicated to many gods

iii   *Si monumentum requiris circumspice* 'if you seek his monument, look around you' – the Latin epitaph which the son of the architect Sir Christopher Wren had inscribed on the wall of his masterpiece, St Paul's Cathedral   continued iii **Henry-Georgian** Henry George was an American political writer whose book *Progress and Poverty* (1879) argued that a socialistic society could be brought about by replacing all other taxes by a single one on property

Kropotkinesque Peter Kropotkin was a revolutionary Russian anarchist of the late nineteenth century

like the Sabbath a reference to Mark 2:27

immanent Tao or Logos two names for a spiritual principle which supposedly dwells within and shapes the universe

Brahman divine knowledge

Utilitarianism the principle that an act should be judged by whether it gives the greatest possible good to the greatest number of people

iv **Robert Nichols** a writer better remembered as a poet than as a dramatist. The play referred to is *Wings Over Europe* (1929)

v **Marquis de Sade** a French writer of the 1790s, the era of the French Revolution. His novels record his sexual fantasies. Sadism, achieving sexual pleasure by causing or observing others' pain, is named after him

Robespierre Maximilien de Robespierre was a lawyer who became one of the most extreme leaders of the French Revolution

Babeuf Francois-Noël Babeuf was a French revolutionary who advocated that everyone should have the same income

vi **Thirty Years War** a war involving much of Europe, 1618–48

Bolshevism Communism, the authoritarian, left-wing political movement led by the Soviet government in Russia from 1917

Fascism the authoritarian and nationalist right-wing movements led by Mussolini in Italy and Hitler in Germany

inflation, depression the poor state of the global economy for much of the 1920s and 1930s was a key factor in the rise of Fascism and Communism, as people turned in desperation to extreme political movements which promised decisive remedies for their troubles

Hiroshima the Japanese city on which the first atomic bomb was dropped on 6 August 1945, killing and maiming more than 130,000 people

CHECK THE BOOK
There are detailed accounts of the historical period in Eric Hobsbawm's *Age of Extremes: The Short Twentieth Century, 1914–1991* (1994) and Mark Mazower's *Dark Continent: Europe's Twentieth Century* (1998).

vi   **Magdeburg** a German city which was destroyed, and its inhabitants massacred, in 1631, during the Thirty Years' War

vii   **Procrustes** a character in Greek mythology who made guests fit his bed by either stretching them or cutting off their legs

         totalitarian governments those which control all aspects of their citizens' lives and tolerate no opposition

         statism state control of everyone's lives

         the sin against the Holy Ghost the worst of crimes

viii   **Jesuits** a Roman Catholic religious order founded in 1534, also known as the Society of Jesus

         Voltaire pen name of the French author François Marie Arouet, best known for his **satire** *Candide* (1759). Although educated by Jesuits, he grew up to be a famous critic of the Church (see **Literary background**)

         'iron curtain' Huxley compares the silence put between people and the truth to the militarised border between capitalist and Communist Europe after the Second World War. Winston Churchill, Britain's prime minister for most of the war years, used the expression 'iron curtain' in a speech on 16 August 1945, and thereafter it became a part of everyday speech until the collapse of European Communism in 1989

         Manhattan Projects Manhattan Project was the code name for the secret US programme to develop an atomic bomb, 1942–5

ix   **scopolamine** a drug, also called hyoscine, which can be used as a sedative

         eugenics the study of inherited characteristics in human beings and the use of this knowledge to improve the health of future generations. In the late nineteenth and early twentieth century, the eugenic movement became associated with racism and the compulsory sterilisation of the mentally disabled. This pseudoscientific programme was to reach its nadir in the Nazis' attempt to exterminate the Jews, since which time the word 'eugenics' has fallen out of general favour (see **Scientific background**, on **Eugenics**)

x   **cannon fodder** soldiers who are regarded as expendable

? QUESTION

Compare the opening one or two chapters of *Brave New World* with the opening of a comparable dystopia, for example Margaret Atwood's *The Handmaid's Tale* (1985) or George Orwell's *Nineteen Eighty-Four* (1949).

CHAPTER 1

- In the year 632 After Ford, a future period when human babies are mass-produced in factories to fit the requirements of society, the Director of the London Hatchery and Conditioning Centre is showing the process to his new students.
- He is assisted by another official, Henry Foster.
- During the tour they meet a nurse called Lenina Crowne, who is one of Henry's lovers.

The opening chapter takes place at the Central London Hatchery and Conditioning Centre in the year AF 632 (by today's reckoning, the middle of the twenty-sixth century). The centre's Director is showing his most recent group of students how human beings are created under laboratory conditions. The group begins in the Fertilizing Room, where human eggs are fertilised and 'bokanovskified' (in effect, cloned) inside test tubes. The Director explains that the aim is to produce 'uniform batches' of men and women (p. 5). He is joined by another official from the centre, Henry Foster, who adds further details to the explanation as they continue.

In the Bottling Room the eggs are transferred into containers and sent along a conveyor belt to the Social Predestination Room, where the destiny of what by this stage are embryos is fixed. The embryos are allocated to one of five basic standards of intelligence (Alphas, Betas, Gammas, Deltas or Epsilons), depending on the predicted needs of society for different types of workers. From the Predestination Room the bottles descend to the Embryo Store, where they are placed in racks and subjected to the conditions which will, when combined with their heredity, produce appropriate types of people, not only in terms of their levels of intelligence, but also in their suitability for the physical climates in which they will work. At this stage, also, hormones are modified to produce the required numbers of males, females and 'freemartins' (sterile females). In the Embryo Store the party encounter a female worker or 'nurse' called Lenina Crowne, who is immunising

CONTEXT

Cloning is the process of creating genetically identical individuals using body cells from an embryo or an adult. The first successful clone was a sheep named Dolly, produced in Scotland in 1997.

embryos against diseases. Henry makes an assignation to meet her on the roof of the centre that afternoon.

COMMENTARY

The opening description of a huge building as 'squat' and 'only' thirty-four storeys in height at once propels us into a world which is disturbingly different to our own. We learn that this is a World State, greater in scale than the mere nation states of the early twentieth century. The first and last words of the World State's motto, 'COMMUNITY, IDENTITY, STABILITY', might seem appealing, but the ambiguity of the middle term indicates the sinister truth, that this future society has been able to achieve solidarity and stability only by minimising its citizens' uniqueness. 'Identity' here refers not to the development of an individual self, but to the state's attempt to make everyone as identical as possible.

The description of the Fertilizing Room (its name and purpose are kept from us until the third paragraph in order to concentrate on the unpleasant details) is strongly negative. The room faces towards the cold north. Words such as 'harsh', 'bleakly', 'wintriness' and 'corpse-coloured' create a chilly mood. The deathly **imagery** is at once reinforced by the description of the light as 'dead, a ghost' (p. 1). Such images recur throughout the book. Later in this chapter people are described as 'spectres' (p. 8) and, again, 'ghosts' (p. 9). By the time the Director appears on the scene, it has been made very clear to us that the Centre is an evil place and we are ready to respond sceptically to the enthusiastic account of it which he gives.

One of the major problems facing any author who writes about an imaginary future is how to convey all the information that the reader needs without turning the story into a series of dull essays. The Director's lecture to the students is an effective device for explaining the artificial breeding of people, but, since it would lack drama if it consisted entirely of talk, Huxley at the same time takes us on a tour of the building, matching explanation with description and with audience reaction from the students. He speeds up and enlivens the process by adding Henry Foster as a second speaker and by including summaries of the speakers' points by the narrator.

www. CHECK THE NET
To find out how close modern science is to producing batches of identical people, search for the latest information at **http://www. newscientist.com**

At times this varied narration makes it difficult to decide whose words or point of view we are hearing. For example, 'not in piddling twos and threes' (p. 4) may be the Director's scornful description of naturally produced twins and triplets, but it may equally be the narrator giving **sarcastic** expression to the Director's underlying thoughts. The phrase 'you will agree' in the previous line is probably the Director's remark to the students, but by taking it out of speech marks, Huxley transfers the pronoun 'you' from the students to us, raising the question of whether we wish to agree with the Director. This indeterminacy of narrator is typical of the book. One effect of it is to focus our attention on the world being described as much as on the characters who are talking about it. Another effect is to make us unsure where the opinions we read are coming from, forcing us to stay alert and sceptical about them.

Huxley increases the pace and the credibility of his explanations by avoiding a formal style in which points are explained fully one after another. Instead, he uses **minor sentences** and **ellipsis** ('Mature at six; the elephant at ten', p. 12) to create a matter-of-fact tone. The words 'always' almost at the end of the chapter's fourth paragraph (p. 2) and 'would' in the next section ('he would explain to them') make it clear that the Director's speech is a set one which he gives regularly. No less than the manufacture of people on the production line, the Director's speech and all the other events in this chapter are part of a mechanical cycle which repeats over and over without significant change.

The production line typifies the system of manufacture pioneered early in the twentieth century by the car maker Henry Ford: a system in which jobs are broken down into components and sequenced one after another so that comparatively unskilled workers can assemble uniform products for the mass market, repetitiously but with maximum efficiency. As Charlie Chaplin was to do shortly afterwards in his **satirical** film *Modern Times* (1936), Huxley begins his story by focusing on this process. What is revolutionary about his approach is that he does not simply show human beings enslaved to the limited, machine-like activities of industrial production, but human beings who are themselves the products of the production line, standardised into Alphas, Betas and so on, almost as though they were a range of cars or bottled drinks.

CHECK THE FILM

Charlie Chaplin's *Modern Times* (1936) shows the 'little man' struggling against aspects of the modern world.

The book's opening chapter suggests that the techniques revolutionising twentieth-century industry may in time be applied to human reproduction and education, on the basis that whatever rational planning and scientific techniques human beings apply to the external world, they will eventually apply to themselves. Huxley envisages the outcome if inappropriate industrial techniques were adopted as the model for all civilisation, with human beings manufactured to set specifications, some people deliberately bred to be infertile, and unethical experiments carried out on others, like the people at Mombassa who are made sexually mature at four. While Huxley's confident use of scientific vocabulary helps to make the twenty-sixth-century breeding and programming process seem convincing, the nineteenth- and twentieth-century names which he drops into his account (Podsnap, Pilkington and an irreverently feminised Lenin) seem comically out of place and alert us to his satirical intention. What we are reading is not so much a sober prediction of the future as a **witty** comment on contemporary trends.

Compared to the enormities of the production line for babies, the characters we meet in Chapter 1 make relatively little impact. However, we note the smugness of the Director, the unintelligent passivity of the students, and the surprising relationship between Foster and Lenina, and we end the opening section of the book ready to learn more, particularly about this odd friendship.

CHECK THE BOOK
In his article 'Prophecies of Fascism', George Orwell commented that 'although *Brave New World* was a brilliant caricature of the present (the present of 1930), it probably casts no light on the future'.

GLOSSARY

1	**lay figure** artist's model
2	**in this year of stability, A.F. 632** instead of numbering years from the time of Jesus and referring to each of them as 'the year of our Lord' (or, in Latin, *Anno Domini*), the citizens of the future number their years from the era when the American car maker Henry Ford transformed industry by introducing the moving assembly line (at some point between 1908 and 1913)
3	**thermogene** medicated cotton wool
	Bokanovsky the names used in *Brave New World* generally refer to people who shaped modern society or social thought. The degree of this influence varies greatly, as does certainty of identification. Bokanovsky has been

continued

linked to Maurice Bokanowski, a French minister of commerce who died in an air crash in 1928, but also to Ivan Vasilevich Bokanowsky, a Russian revolutionary

4 **the old viviparous days** when humans still gave birth to children

5 **mass production** the use of standardised methods to manufacture anything in large amounts

Podsnap's Technique Mr Podsnap is a character in Charles Dickens's novel *Our Mutual Friend* (1865) who has narrow fixed views on everything, including how to raise his daughter, and who disposes of problems by denying their existence

6 **Mr Foster** Henry Foster's first name is presumably intended to recall Henry Ford. For his surname, Huxley may have had in mind Sir Michael Foster, the scientist who succeeded his grandfather T. H. Huxley as professor of physiology at the Royal Institution

pituitary extract from a gland which influences several bodily processes, including growth

sow's peritoneum membrane lining a pig's abdomen

7 **Matriculators** since 'to matriculate' means to be enrolled into a college, generally by examination, it is likely that these machines check the eggs' quality and reject those which fail the test

morula the ball of cells which a fertilised egg becomes as it divides

8 **lupus** a skin disease which causes a red, blotchy rash on the face

9 **placentin** presumably, a substance which nourishes the embryo with the chemicals which would normally have been supplied by the mother's placenta (see below)

thyroxin a growth hormone produced by the thyroid gland

corpus luteum a hormone-producing body which maintains the lining of the uterus ready for fertilisation

placenta usually the organ which links the blood supply of a baby to that of its mother, so nourishing it and allowing it to breathe; here, a mechanical substitute for that organ

10 **'trauma of decanting'** the Austrian psychoanalyst Otto Rank suggested in 1924 that being born is a shock or

CONTEXT

Aldous Huxley's grandfather, Thomas Henry Huxley (1825–95), was one of the leading scientific figures of his day, champion of science teaching and working-class education, author of influential essays and textbooks, coiner of the word 'agnostic' and, above all, chief public advocate of the theory of evolution by natural selection or, in his own words, 'Darwin's bulldog'.

'trauma' which can affect the later development of the personality

10   **freemartins** usually, creatures born with a mixture of male and female organs; here, sterile females

12   **endocrine** gland releasing hormones directly into the bloodstream

postulated a germinal mutation suggested that the slow growth of human beings was caused by some deviation in their early development

Pilkington the name recalls the British glass-making company Pilkington, whose products included vitaglass, which permitted the passage of ultraviolet light and which is referred to in Chapter 11

13   **Lenina** her name recalls Vladimir Lenin, the Communist leader who seized power in Russia in 1917

14   **The embryos still have gills** human embryos pass through a fish-like stage in which they have gills and a tail

CHAPTER 2

- The tour continues.
- The Director shows the students how the babies' feelings are trained by conditioning and sleep-indoctrination so that they will grow up with the attitudes required by the World State.

 CHECK THE BOOK

Jerry W. Carlson in his essay 'Aldous Huxley' in *Dictionary of Literary Biography*, Vol. 36 (1985), says: 'It is no accident that Huxley begins by describing an institution rather than by focusing on the actions or attributes of a protagonist.' *Brave New World* portrays a society rather than individualised characters.

Henry Foster remains in the Decanting Room. The other members of the party proceed to the fifth floor, where infants are equipped with the attitudes that the World State deems appropriate. The students see how eight-month-old Deltas are taught to hate books and flowers by associating them with loud noises and electric shocks. The painful conditioning not only deters members of this low caste from reading anything which might disrupt their Delta mentality, but also prevents them from spending time admiring the countryside when they could be more profitably occupied supporting the economy by consuming manufactured goods. The students next see how children are indoctrinated in their sleep.

The Director explains that it has proved difficult to transmit factual information effectively by whispering it over and over, but 'hypnopaedia' (p. 21) has nonetheless been successfully used to encourage social prejudices, making each caste happy with its own way of life and hostile towards others'. He becomes so exultant in his explanation of this that he inadvertently wakes up the children.

COMMENTARY

Chapter 1 leaves the reader in a mixed mood, increasingly horrified, yet also amused by the casual, **satirical** tone with which the horrors are described. Chapter 2 continues and intensifies both parts of this reaction.

QUESTION

How does Huxley attempt to introduce comedy into *Brave New World*, and to what extent does he succeed in making the novel amusing?

A **slapstick** quality broadens the humour. The trick played on the toddlers, the embarrassment of the students at talking about things which are normal to us but which to them have become taboo subjects, and the Director's blunder in waking the children with his enthusiastic speechifying are all portrayed in a light-hearted way, yet we can hardly overlook that what we are seeing is monstrously cruel. The helpless infants are terrorised by electric shocks and loud sounds and, as a result, cut off from books and natural beauty for the rest of their lives. Their minds are closed and their reasoning powers bypassed by the use of sleep-teaching. The individual's capacity to form a view of life based on personal experience is replaced by 'Suggestions from the State' (p. 25).

Once again, the pace and informality of the explanations help retain our interest, especially since the second chapter is more dramatic than the first, with the infants all too clearly illustrating the Director's point when they are made to suffer. Brackets are used to add brisk commentary, so that we move rapidly from one level of narration to another. Once this technique is established, the narrative can become remarkably fluid. When we and the students are told about experiments in sleep-teaching, for example, Huxley abandons the Director's voice and presents the incidents directly as part of the story.

The satirical element of the book also becomes more prominent in the second chapter, particularly through the references to Henry Ford.

(See **Text 1** of **Extended commentaries** for further discussion of part of this chapter.)

GLOSSARY

16   **Neo-Pavlovian** the Russian scientist Ivan Pavlov showed in 1903 that animal behaviour can be changed by training (or 'conditioning') a reflex so that it responds to a stimulus which would not normally affect it. In this chapter the babies' natural fear of pain and noise is artificially extended to the sight of books and flowers

      Aryan a supposed Indo-European racial grouping (see **Scientific background**, on **Eugenics**)

      quartos books

18   **What man has joined, nature is powerless to put asunder** 'What therefore God hath joined together, let no man put asunder' (Mark 10:9), a saying familiar not only from the Bible but from the Anglican marriage service

20   **Our Ford** in this secular world, the life of Henry Ford has replaced that of 'Our Lord' Jesus as the most significant era in history

      smut obscene talk about sex

21   **George Bernard Shaw** one of the greatest dramatists and humorous writers of the twentieth century; also a self-publicist who admired the dictatorships of Lenin and Mussolini and who predicted the evolution of human beings into 'supermen'

      T-Model Ford's Model T, which began production in 1908, was the first car made for the mass market

      a sign of the T the Director makes this sign when he speaks of Henry Ford, as Christians sometimes make the sign of the cross when they speak of God

23   **categorical imperative** a term coined by the German philosopher Immanuel Kant in 1797 to describe an absolute moral law, such as 'treat others as you believe they should treat you'; here, it merely refers to the order to be silent

      Class Consciousness a term used by followers of the socialist thinker Karl Marx to describe an awareness of belonging to a social class which has important conflicts of interest with others; here, in contrast, it merely means an awareness that members of a social class should behave in certain ways to conform to society's needs

---

CONTEXT

George Bernard Shaw (1856–1950) produced his own version of a future society in his 1921 play *Back to Methuselah*, in which the human lifespan is drastically extended.

CHAPTER 3

- The Resident Controller for Western Europe, Mustapha Mond, joins the group and tells the students why such a highly regulated society was developed.
- Elsewhere in the Centre, Lenina is discussing her social life with her friend Fanny. Fanny disapproves of Lenina's four-month relationship with Henry Foster, which goes against the custom of promiscuity.
- Lenina responds by expressing interest in Bernard Marx, whose stunted appearance causes many of his colleagues to regard him as abnormal.
- Bernard, meanwhile, longs for Lenina but is repelled by the society in which he lives.

CONTEXT

The concept of 'infantile sexuality' – that young children go through phases of sexual feeling and behaviour as part of their normal development – was one of the many influential ideas put forward by Sigmund Freud (1856–1939). With his customary scorn of Freud, Huxley exaggerates the notion here for satirical effect.

The Director takes the students out into the garden of the Centre to watch the children playing in the summer sunshine. He comments on their games, which have to be played with elaborate manufactured toys in order to promote consumption, and on their erotic activities, which it is clear that one little boy does not like. The Director reveals to the incredulous students that sexual behaviour in children was at one time suppressed, rather than encouraged.

At this point the group is joined by Mustapha Mond, Resident Controller for Western Europe, who elaborates upon this contrast between past and present. He describes how the family and monogamy, along with Christianity, poverty and ageing, were features of the past which led to strong personal feelings. After the violent disruption of a Nine Years' War, social stability became the world's overwhelming priority. It was at first pursued by attempting to abolish culture, historical awareness and religion forcibly, but this policy provoked resistance. It proved more effective to eradicate them by developing a society based on compulsory consumption and the universal availability of sex and euphoric drugs, producing a world in which no one could experience sustained frustration or any other mental state liable to foster self-awareness and initiative.

The speeches of the Director and Mond are intercut with events taking place elsewhere, which illustrate their points but which at the same time show that the system is not yet totally effective.

In the Girls' Dressing-Room of the Centre, Lenina is discussing her social life with Fanny, a friend who shares her surname Crowne (presumably because she originally came from the same batch of genetic material). Fanny disapproves of Lenina's four-month relationship with Henry Foster, which goes against the norm of promiscuity. Lenina responds by expressing interest in Bernard Marx, an Alpha-Plus from the Psychology Bureau who has invited her to accompany him to a Savage Reservation.

CHECK THE BOOK
The ideas of Karl Marx (from whom Bernard Marx derives his name) are helpfully explained and assessed in *Marx: A Very Short Introduction* by Peter Singer (1980).

Fanny thinks Bernard unsuitable because he is stunted in appearance and he spends an abnormal amount of time by himself. There are rumours that his development may have been spoiled by an accidental injection of alcohol while he was in the bottle. Lenina dismisses this accusation, however, and says that in any case she has always wanted to visit a Reservation.

Meanwhile, Bernard is experiencing the contempt of his fellow workers, Henry Foster and the Assistant Predestinator, who anger him by casual talk about their sexual experiences with Lenina and Fanny. While these three sets of conversations are taking place, the production line of babies continues to roll onwards.

COMMENTARY

Chapter 3 is a transitional chapter. It moves from explaining the ideas behind the World State to presenting the experiences of individual characters. In order to do so, it switches with increasing speed between locations and is therefore the most formally adventurous chapter of the book. The tour of the Centre continues with an excursion into the garden and a meeting with Mond the Controller, but it is repeatedly interrupted to follow the lives of Bernard and Lenina. We learn enough about all three characters to make us interested in them and prepare us for later developments. Mond, for example, is rumoured to have forbidden books hidden in a safe; we learn more of these in Chapter 17.

Mond's speech to the students is the central element of the present chapter. It is juxtaposed with dramatised reports of his subject matter, Lenina's conversations with Fanny, and Bernard's conversations with Henry and the Assistant Predestinator. While some of these juxtapositions illustrate Mond's ideas, some imply an ironic commentary. We hear that the family and motherhood have been abolished, and we accordingly see Lenina and Fanny talking about Pregnancy Substitute, but we also see that Lenina and Bernard deviate from the norms which Mond has laid down by giving some signs of a thwarted desire for monogamy.

 CHECK THE BOOK
Jerry W. Carlson in his essay 'Aldous Huxley' in *Dictionary of Literary Biography*, Vol. 36 (1985), says that one of the novel's chief rhetorical strategies is to make the reader recognise what most of the characters cannot grasp: 'that preserving freedom and diversity is necessary to avoid suffering the repressions fostered by shallow ideas of progress'.

At first the movement between the strands of narrative is quite easy to follow, but as the chapter progresses, the sections become shorter and shorter, until they are switching over every two or three lines. The rapid pace is both exhilarating and bewildering, leaving the reader feeling immersed in a fast-moving, alien world with which it is hard to come to terms. This reinforces our situation as visitors to the imaginary world of the future and anticipates the feelings of John later in the story.

There is still an enormous amount of information conveyed in this chapter. In particular, we learn of the Nine Years' War and glimpse something of the process by which this new society came into being. In their ignorance of the past the people of the future have confused Ford and Freud, but the merger also implies that the two men's ideas have something in common: their conception of the individual as a kind of mechanism which can be adjusted by experts to fit the requirements of society.

The kaleidoscope of voices with which Chapter 3 finishes also marks the end of the book's introductory section, which tells us about the basic conditions of the future society. Having glimpsed the growing relationship between Bernard and Lenina, we are ready, once a more normal narrative structure resumes, to follow its development. The final section of Chapter 3, however, reminds us of the underlying nature of this society by bringing us back to the **image** of the production line relentlessly processing its human load.

(See **Text 2** of **Extended commentaries** for a more detailed discussion of part of this chapter.)

GLOSSARY

26	**soliloquized in the boskage** sang to themselves in the trees (the old-fashioned poetic style is deliberately out of place)
27	**Polly Trotsky** the name recalls Leon Trotsky, the Russian revolutionary who, because he opposed the policies of Josef Stalin, was expelled from the Soviet Union in 1929 and later assassinated
28	**auto-erotism** masturbation
29	**his fordship** 'your Lordship' is the title used when speaking to a lord or a judge; here it has been adapted for the Fordian era
	Mustapha Mond the name recalls two modernising leaders of the early twentieth century: Mustafa Kemal, who, as Kemal Ataturk, became founder and first president of the Turkish Republic (1923–38); and Sir Alfred Mond, later Baron Melchett, government minister, philanthropist and (in 1928) co-founder and first chairman of Imperial Chemical Industries
	Discarnate disembodied
	Bernard Marx his last name recalls the German economic philosopher Karl Marx, the most influential of socialist thinkers and writers, whose sustained and principled discontent with nineteenth-century society contrasts with his namesake's mere petulance. Bernard's first name may be meant to recall Claude Bernard, another nineteenth-century figure, a French physiologist whose work on the self-regulation of the body helped establish the principles of experimental research
30	**History is bunk** Henry Ford famously dismissed the past in 1916 with the words 'History is more or less bunk' (i.e. worthless)
	Harappa ... Ur ... Thoughts of Pascal a catalogue of cultural knowledge. Harappa, Ur, Thebes, Knossos and Mycenae are ancient centres of culture, Odysseus is the Greek hero whose adventures are recounted in Homer's *Odyssey*, Job a biblical hero who endures terrible suffering, Jupiter a Roman god, Gotama (or Gautama) the founder of Buddhism, the Middle Kingdom one of the states of China, *King Lear* one of Shakespeare's great tragedies, and the *Thoughts* of Blaise Pascal a book by a notable mathematician, scientist and religious thinker of seventeenth-century France

continued

CHECK THE BOOK

George Orwell's *Nineteen Eighty-Four* (1949) and Margaret Atwood's *The Handmaid's Tale* (1985) are later dystopias which can be compared to *Brave New World*.

CHAPTER 3 continued

CHECK THE BOOK
There is a detailed discussion of H.G. Wells's influence on Huxley in Chapter 6 of *The Future as Nightmare: H.G. Wells and the Anti-Utopians* by Mark R. Hillegas (1967).

30 Passion a musical expression of Christ's suffering on the cross

Requiem a musical setting of the church service for the souls of the dead

Feelies pornographic film which make use of the sense of touch (when Huxley was writing, the 'talkies' had recently replaced silent films)

the Alhambra the original Alhambra is a thirteenth-century Moorish palace in Granada, Spain; in twentieth-century Britain luxurious cinemas often adopted its name

32 periodically teeming regularly becoming pregnant

33 Dr Wells the name recalls H. G. Wells (1866–1946), the writer whose **science fiction** and **utopian** ideas are in part continued, in part mocked, by *Brave New World* (see **Literary background** and **Critical approaches**, on **Intertextuality**)

Pregnancy Substitute medication used to prevent any disturbance of the female body and mind caused by the unavailability of pregnancy

34 Our Freud Sigmund Freud was an Austrian psychiatrist who from the 1890s developed an approach to mental disturbance called psychoanalysis, based on the idea that many mental disorders originate in repressed sexual desires. Although in recent times much of his work has been called into question, it was remarkably fashionable for much of the twentieth century (see **Themes**)

Samoa … New Guinea … the Trobriands islands in the Pacific Ocean, whose societies had been analysed in several well-known books of the 1920s by two pioneering anthropologists, the American Margaret Mead and Bronislaw Malinowski, a Briton. Their findings were taken to demonstrate how different from one another societies could be, suggesting an extreme flexibility to human nature, but have not always been supported by later investigators

39 flivver an inexpensive motor car. The saying **parodies** well-known lines from Robert Browning's 1841 poem 'Pippa Passes': 'God's in His heaven – / All's right with the world'

pneumatic inflated by compressed air, a **metaphor** for 'generously curved', derived from T. S. Eliot's 1918 poem 'Whispers of Immortality': 'her friendly bust / Gives promise of pneumatic bliss'

41   **Ectogenesis** the creation of a child outside the mother's body

Pfitzner the name recalls the German composer Hans Pfitzner, who opposed modernism in music during the first half of the twentieth century

Kawaguchi Shramana Ekai Kawaguchi was a Japanese monk, whose book *Three Years in Tibet* Huxley had reviewed in his essay collection, *On the Margin* (1923)

42   **Phosgene, chloropicrin … hydrocyanic acid** poisonous substances, supposedly used in the Nine Years' War

Kurfurstendamm one of the main streets of Berlin

Eighth Arrondissement a district of Paris

anthrax bombs anthrax is a potentially fatal disease, normally confined to livestock, but occasionally spread to humans

$CH_3C_6H_2(NO_2)_3 + Hg(CNO)_2$ the formula for the explosive TNT, plus the formula for mercuric fulminate, a detonator

44   **Simple Lifers** people who reject lifestyles which are dependent upon sophisticated machinery and mass consumption

Golders Green a north London suburb

45   **Malthusian belt** a belt for carrying contraceptives. In 1798 the economist Thomas Malthus had argued that the poor would remain poor unless they succeeded in limiting the number of children they had. Later advocates of birth control were therefore known as Malthusians

46   **bandolier** a shoulder belt for carrying ammunition (or in this case, contraceptives)

fixation of nitrogen turning the gas nitrogen into a solid

48   *soma* the original soma was an intoxicating drink used in Hindu religious rituals in late eighteenth-century India

Hoity-toity a slang expression (also 'highty-tighty') indicating bad temper

Gonadal hormones chemicals produced by the sex glands

49   **physiological stigmata** bodily signs

CONTEXT

Huxley stated in an interview that 'Soma is an imaginary drug, with three different effects – euphoric, hallucinant, or sedative – an impossible combination.'

CHAPTER 4

- Lenina agrees in principle to go with Bernard to a Savage Reservation, then sets off for a game of Obstacle Golf with Henry.
- Bernard goes to visit Helmholtz Watson, a friend with whom he is able to share some of his misgivings about the nature of modern society.

Lenina sees Bernard in the lift to the roof of the Centre, and tells him that she would be pleased to visit the Savage Reservation with him for a week in July. She rather enjoys the shock of other men in the lift that she is willing to go with Bernard, though Bernard himself is clearly embarrassed by their conversation and disgusted when one of her former lovers, Benito Hoover, attempts to engage him in banter afterwards. While Henry Foster flies Lenina across London in his helicopter for a game of Obstacle Golf, Bernard pilots his plane to the roof of Propaganda House, where his friend Helmholtz Watson works as an 'emotional engineer' (p. 59), producing scripts for radio and writing feelies. Whereas all his life Bernard's inferior physique has caused him to feel different from others, it is only recently that Helmholtz has realised that the success brought by his good looks and talent has left him wanting something more. The pair fly to Bernard's home, where they can privately discuss their dissatisfactions with society. Helmholtz reveals that he feels badly constrained as a writer by the limited subject matter of his work.

 CHECK THE NET
Use a comprehensive online encyclopedia such as **http://en.wikipedia.org** to learn about the theories of selective breeding and eugenics.

COMMENTARY

Having outlined the nature of the future society in the first three chapters of the book, Huxley now introduces a pair of contrasting characters who share some of our disgust at it – one motivated by 'mental excess' (p. 60), the other by physical deficiency – and who put forward views for us to consider. However, because they are people who have grown up in the World State, their perspective is not quite the same as our own.

Helmholtz is a highly successful person who develops some limited but telling criticisms of his society based on his needs as a writer. Bernard is a misfit, in some ways inferior to those around him, more motivated by jealousy than idealism. His character is firmly established through contrast with Helmholtz and with Henry. Henry Foster is efficient and confident on his air journey, Bernard irritable and neurotically self-conscious. The two air flights also give us a glimpse of the world beyond the Hatchery and afford Huxley the opportunity for general **satire**, likening the tall buildings to fungus and the people around them to maggots and ants, and showing us areas devoted to the distractions and propaganda which help to prevent people questioning the nature of their society.

A modern reader may feel it is significant that the men pilot the aircraft and the women are passengers. While some feminist readers have responded positively to the World State's destruction of the family, it is certainly not a **utopia** of women's liberation. All the most powerful characters are men and, from the moment the Director pats Lenina in Chapter 1, it is clear that men are meant to take the initiative in personal relations.

CHECK THE BOOK

Jane Deery, Deanna Madden and Elaine Baruch have all questioned the representation of women in the novel.

GLOSSARY

51	**George Edzel** Henry Ford's son was named Edsel
	parathyroid a hormone which helps control the level of calcium in the blood (not the size of the ears)
	Benito Hoover the name recalls the Italian Fascist dictator Benito Mussolini (in power 1922–43) and the US president Herbert Hoover (in power 1929–33)
52	**Charing-T** Charing Cross is the site of one of London's main railway stations
55	**stays** supporting wires between the wings
	planes wings
	Riemann-surface a geometrical surface of several layers, invented by the German mathematician Bernhard Riemann
56	**Television Corporation** television had been developed in the late 1920s, but it was only in 1936, four years after *Brave New World* appeared, that the world's

continued

CHAPTER 4 continued

? QUESTION

Nicholas Murray claims in *Aldous Huxley: An English Intellectual* (2002) that 'The compliant consumers of 2001, loyally obeying brand *diktats*, against a background in which the politics of radical protest are increasingly neutered or abandoned, would strike a contemporary Huxley as a grim vindication.' Do you agree that our society is coming to resemble that of *Brave New World*, and why?

first television service was launched by the British Broadcasting Corporation

56   **Stoke Poges** a village to the west of London with a golf course. Its churchyard is also the burial place of the poet Thomas Gray, and the probable setting of his 'Elegy' (1750), a poem which pays tribute to the lives of ordinary people. The use of this location implies a comparison and contrast between the Romantic past and the mechanistic future

58   **Fleet Street** the London street where most national newspapers had their headquarters at this time

59   ***The Delta Mirror*** the name recalls the popular newspaper, the *Daily Mirror*

Helmholtz Watson Herman von Helmholtz was a German physicist who made a wide range of contributions to science in the second half of the nineteenth century. J. B. Watson was a psychologist whose behaviourist approach dominated the field in America in the 1920s. Watson believed that human actions should be understood in terms of conditioned reflexes (see 'Neo-Pavlovian', Chapter 2), discounting the influence of reason and imagination (see also **Themes**)

CHAPTER 5

- Lenina and Henry go to a multisensory concert, Bernard to a Solidarity Service.
- Both events are designed to merge the individual into a greater whole.

Lenina and Henry fly back from their game of Obstacle Golf. The sight of a crematorium leads them to discuss the meaning of life and the respective value of the different social classes. They eat in a communal dining hall, taking the drug *soma* with their coffee, then go to a concert designed to appeal not only to the sense of hearing, but also to those of sight and smell. Afterwards they return to Henry's room for sex.

Bernard, meanwhile, after dining at Helmholtz's club, has taken an aerial taxi to a Community Singery for his fortnightly attendance at a Solidarity Service. In this equivalent of a religious rite, the participants sing hymns and share *soma* in order to feel part of the 'Greater Being' (p. 72), finally dancing and shouting in an intoxicated procession. As usual, however, Bernard fails to experience the transformation and has to pretend to ecstasy, leaving him bitter and guilty at his sense of exclusion.

COMMENTARY

The sunset with which the chapter opens contrasts with the sunset at the same spot seven hundred years earlier when Thomas Gray wrote his 'Elegy'. As Gray in his poem reflected on the death of an unknown villager who lies buried in Stoke Poges churchyard, so Henry and Lenina reflect on the unknown Alpha or Epsilon whose gases are expelled from the chimney of Slough Crematorium. We might expect Huxley to use this contrast to suggest the different outlooks of the two periods, but surprisingly it serves more to suggest continuity. Having previously evoked horror at the world of the future, Huxley here stresses its resemblance to the world of the twentieth century, making his readers question their own customs and leaving us unsure how to react to the events portrayed. When Lenina recites the slogan 'Everyone's happy now' (p. 67), which was repeated to her eighteen hundred times in her youth through sleep-teaching, we perceive the **irony** of the assertion, but we must then consider whether the ways in which her society seeks happiness are so very different from those of our own.

CHECK THE BOOK

Thomas Gray's 'Elegy' (1751) is a poem that reflects on the lives of ordinary people, who may have had similar qualities to those who became famous, but were never noticed because of their low social class.

Henry and Lenina's visit to the cabaret in Westminster Abbey is a caricature of a twentieth-century evening on the town. The use of drugs other than alcohol as a way of augmenting the experience would have been unusual in most sections of society at the time the book was written, but has become less uncommon in recent times. Our personal reaction to their happiness when they come home 'bottled' and enjoy casual sex is worth considering. Do we condemn them as immoral? Do we envy them? Is our reaction made up of a mixture of feelings?

The secular pleasures of food, drink, drugs, music, dancing and sex are followed by the religious communion of the Solidarity Service.

Karl Marx
(1818–83) was
an atheist who
believed that
religion expressed
real human needs
but in a perverted
form. He wrote:
'Religion is the
sigh of the
oppressed
creature, the
heart of a
heartless world ...
It is the opium of
the people. The
abolition of
religion as the
illusory happiness
of the people is
required for their
real happiness.'

This travesty of a Christian service is likely to outrage a religious believer, with the twelve participants recalling the twelve apostles, and the *soma* and ice cream replacing the bread and wine. (The scene perhaps dramatises Karl Marx's famous comment, 'Religion ... is the opium of the people'.) However, with the exception of Bernard, the congregation do seem to experience feelings of transcendence, and there is no apparent irony in the descriptions of Fifi as having achieved a 'rich and living peace' (p. 76).

The element of **parody** in Huxley's descriptions invites us to condemn the customs of the future as absurd rituals ('twelve buttocks slabbily resounding', p. 75), but at the same time the resemblance to a present-day night out and a church service suggests that our own behaviour might seem equally absurd to a detached observer. With this chapter, the book passes from relatively simple **satire** to a more challenging reading experience which requires us to think about our reactions more deeply.

GLOSSARY

64 **Internal and External Secretions Trust** a farming company which takes both hormones and milk from cows. The reference to the 'lowing' of the cows recalls the second line of Gray's 'Elegy' (see 'Stoke Poges', Chapter 4): 'the lowing herd winds slowly o'er the lea'

65 **Slough Crematorium** due to the building of a large trading estate in the 1920s, the town of Slough was growing rapidly at the time that Huxley was writing. John Betjeman's 1937 poem 'Slough' was to single it out as typical of the ugliness of mass society

67 **Westminster Abbey Cabaret** the central place of worship of the Anglican Church, where British kings and queens were crowned, has become a restaurant featuring entertainment acts

Calvin Stopes the name recalls John Calvin, the sixteenth-century French Protestant reformer who claimed that God had predestined everyone to be saved or damned; and Marie Stopes, the early twentieth-century birth-control pioneer

Sexophonists the saxophone became a popular musical instrument between the world wars, associated with jazz and dancing, and therefore also with freedom in sexual behaviour

67 **Bottle of mine** the title and lyric recall 'Dear Old Pal of Mine', an American song of 1918, still well known at the time the book was written

68 **the little death** orgasm

deturgescence emptying out of something bloated and swollen

70 **Aphroditæum** a club named after Aphrodite, the Greek goddess of love. The name recalls (and contrasts with) the Athenæum, a prominent London club to which Huxley belonged, and also the *Athenæum* magazine to which he was a contributor, both named after Athene, the Greek goddess of wisdom

Fordson Community Singery a replacement for St Paul's Cathedral, which stands at the head of Ludgate Hill

Carrara-surrogate imitation of the world's finest marble

Big Henry Big Ben is the bell of the clock in the Houses of Parliament, but the name is often applied to the clock itself. In the era of Henry Ford, the most famous clock in London is named after him and is not associated with elected government

71 **Morgana Rothschild** the name recalls two wealthy dynasties. The Pierpoint Morgans were powerful American businessmen in the first half of the twentieth century; the Rothschilds, a highly successful family of bankers from the eighteenth to the twentieth centuries

Fifi Bradlaugh Charles Bradlaugh was a journalist and politician who advocated birth control and atheism and who was denied his seat in Parliament for five years in the 1880s because he refused to take the customary religious oath

Joanna Diesel Rudolf Diesel, a German engineer, developed the diesel engine during the 1890s

Clara Deterding Clara Bryant was Henry Ford's wife. Henri Deterding was a powerful Dutch oil magnate, notorious for his efforts to keep the price of oil high and for subsidising Hitler in the hope that the Germans would invade Russia and recapture the oil wells which the Soviets had taken from him

Tom Kawaguchi see Kawaguchi, Chapter 3

CHECK THE BOOK

A fascinating account of pre-twentieth-century communitarian experiments is Mark Holloway's *Heavens on Earth: Utopian Communities in America, 1680–1880* (1966). Holloway conveys the sense of boundless hope that drove these experiments.

CONTEXT

Mikhail Bakunin pointed out the danger of a Marxist revolution producing a ruling elite who, although claiming to represent the will of the people, would actually run society in their own interests.

71	**Sarojini Engels** Mrs Sarojini Naidu was an Indian politician whom Huxley had met in Bombay in 1925. Friedrich Engels, the German socialist author, collaborated with Karl Marx on the *Communist Manifesto* of 1848
	Herbert Bakunin Mikhail Bakunin was a Russian anarchist who opposed Marx's version of socialism in the 1860s. Huxley may also have had in mind the British philosopher Herbert Spencer, who in the second half of the nineteenth century attempted to produce a comprehensive philosophy founded on Darwin's work on evolution
72	**bowels of compassion** a biblical phrase, from the First Epistle of John 3:17
	'Come, Greater Being' based on a seventeenth-century hymn
75	**'Orgy-porgy'** the song is an adaptation of the nursery rhyme 'Georgie Porgie, pudding and pie / Kissed the girls and made them cry. / When the boys came out to play, / Georgie Porgie ran away'

CHAPTER 6

- Lenina is disturbed by Bernard's unorthodox attitudes, but she remains intrigued by the opportunity he offers her to visit a Savage Reservation.
- Bernard gets the permit for their visit initialled by the Director, who reveals that he once went there with a girl who became lost and was never seen again.
- The Director is embarrassed at his personal disclosure and, once Bernard and Lenina have gone to New Mexico, he begins plotting to exile Bernard to Iceland.

Lenina finds Bernard's unorthodox attitudes disturbing. He likes to be with her in natural surroundings, not in a crowd; to talk to her, not just sleep with her; and to experience the reality of a bad mood, rather than be anaesthetised against it by *soma*. Only the unique opportunity to visit a Savage Reservation persuades her to continue with his company.

Bernard has to get his permit to visit the reservation in New Mexico initialled by the Director. Uncharacteristically, the Director breaks with convention by confiding some details of his past, telling Bernard that almost twenty-five years ago he too went there with a girl. They became separated in a thunderstorm and, injured, he left without her, assuming that she had been killed. The experience still haunts his dreams, but he denies any abnormal attachment to the girl and tries to distract attention from his emotional 'weakness' by criticising Bernard's behaviour outside working hours. Bernard is quite pleased by this attack, which makes him feel important. He reports it in an exaggerated way to Helmholtz, who is embarrassed by Bernard's boasting and self-pity.

Bernard and Lenina fly to New Mexico, where they are told details of the Savage Reservation by its Warden. Bernard remembers that he has left a scent tap running in his bathroom at home and rings Helmholtz to ask him to turn it off. He is dismayed when Helmholtz reveals that the Director is now openly planning to exile him to Iceland. Bernard and Lenina finally arrive at the Reservation by plane.

COMMENTARY

Bernard has now become the central figure of the story. In the first part of the chapter, he is contrasted with Lenina, bringing out his unorthodoxy; in the second part, with the Director and, to a lesser extent, with Helmholtz, making clear how conventional he in some ways remains.

Bernard's quarrels with Lenina are liable to arouse our sympathy for his point of view, but if his opinions are superior to hers, they certainly do not raise the standard of his behaviour. His attitude towards her is uncaring and even bullying. We notice this the more because so much of their debate is seen from Lenina's point of view. Placing a greater emphasis on character than previously, Huxley makes use of free indirect discourse to let us see events through the eyes of individuals. For example, the chapter gets off to a lively start

CHECK THE FILM

In Michael R. Joyce's 1998 film adaptation of *Brave New World*, entry to the Reservation is forbidden, and it is inhabited by twentieth-century 'trailer trash' Americans who attack the visitors when their helicopter crashes there. Why do you think these major changes were introduced?

by letting us share Lenina's thoughts on Bernard ('Odd, odd, *odd*', p. 78) and the reasoning behind her agreement to go on holiday with him. Later, when he halts the helicopter and forces her to look at the untamed natural world, her subjective perceptions of 'the rushing emptiness of the night' (p. 80) introduce an unusually serious note into the story.

The meeting with the Director is important in the development of the **plot**; we are intrigued by the Director's confessions about his past experience in New Mexico and suspect, rightly, that this will later prove significant. It is **ironic** that Bernard, who likes to think of himself as a rebel against society, is shocked by what the Director tells him. Like the dissent of Bernard and Helmholtz and Lenina's susceptibility to monogamy, the Director's lapse is another hint that, for all its apparatus of conditioning, this brave new world remains at odds with human nature. We side with Bernard in his defiance of the Director, but Helmholtz's reservations about his later boasting ensure that Bernard remains a comic victim, rather than a hero whose outlook we can confidently endorse. Bernard's (false) claim that he told the Director to go to 'the Bottomless Past' (p. 88) – the World State equivalent of 'go to hell' – is an indication that he remains trapped in the outlook of his time, unable to conceive that the past might contain anything worth knowing.

In the third part, the action moves from England to America, and from an artificial, urban world to a primitive, natural one, a point emphasised in the Warden's speech. We wonder how the visitors will cope and, after Bernard's phone call, whether he or the Director will prevail in their coming battle.

CONTEXT

In an interview Huxley explained: 'I had to do an enormous amount of reading up on New Mexico because I'd never been there. I read all sorts of Smithsonian reports on the place and then did the best I could to imagine it. I didn't actually go there until six years later.'

GLOSSARY

78	**Jean-Jacques Habibullah** the name recalls Jean-Jacques Rousseau, the influential French thinker of the eighteenth century who saw the human being as a 'noble savage' corrupted by society, and Habibullah Khan, Amir of Afghanistan from 1901 to 1919, who modernised his country and introduced its first schools and factories
79	**the Oxford Union** home of the University Debating Society
	St Andrews home of the Royal and Ancient Golf Club

90	brachycephalic short-headed
92	half-breeds people of mixed race
	totemism worship of a natural object, such as an animal, as a spiritual symbol
94	octoroon a person who is of one eighth Negro ancestry
	Malpais Spanish for 'bad region', an actual place near the Mexican border
	pueblo a Spanish American Indian village
	mesa a table-shaped hill

CHECK THE BOOK

For an interesting general interview with Huxley, see *Writers at Work: Second Series* (1963), edited by George Plimpton.

CHAPTER 7

- Lenina is shocked by the Indians' primitive way of life.
- After she and Bernard witness a fertility ceremony in which a young man is beaten with whips, they are startled to meet an English-speaking Savage called John.
- He takes them to meet his mother, Linda. She is evidently the woman whom the Director left in the reservation over twenty years before, and John is the Director's son.

A guide takes Bernard and Lenina to the savage village. The strange appearance of its inhabitants and the insanitary conditions there shock Lenina, especially when she sees such unaccustomed sights as a man who is visibly elderly and diseased and women who breast-feed their children. Bernard attempts to praise what he sees, but becomes silent when they witness a fertility ceremony. At its climax a young man of eighteen walks round a pile of live snakes while masked men beat him with whips until he falls. Another young man joins the visitors, lamenting that he was not chosen to be the sacrifice. This newcomer, John, speaks perfect English, though in an unusual style incorporating quotations from Shakespeare, and is obviously attracted to Lenina. He explains that his mother Linda came from outside the Reservation and was trapped there by an accident. Bernard realises that she must be the woman whom the

Director left years before and that John must be the Director's son. John takes the visitors to his home where they meet his mother. Deprived of the aids of civilisation, Linda has turned into a fat, wrinkled woman who oddly mixes the mentality of a savage with that of a homesick Beta. It seems that her promiscuity has made her an outcast among the savages and caused the other children to persecute her son.

COMMENTARY

CONTEXT

The Tewa Indians of New Mexico have mixed Christianity with their own ancient beliefs, celebrating saints' days, for example, with the corn dance or bow and arrow dance. New Mexico is also home to the Hermanos Penitentes, or Penitential Brotherhood, who believe they must experience the pain of Jesus in order to be saved, carrying heavy wooden crosses in their Good Friday procession while beating one another with whips.

Here, Bernard and Lenina enter a world very different from the man-made one with which they are familiar, its closeness to nature symbolised by the eagle which flies so near to them that its wingbeats chill their faces. The primitive society of the pueblo is not, however, held up as superior to the World State. Rather, it is presented as one of many possible variations of human existence. The couple's walk with the Indian guide is a transition between two societies which are not as dissimilar as they may at first seem. The visitors' feet fall into the rhythm of the native drums, but soon Lenina perceives its resemblance to the beat of the Solidarity Service, and the scenic description of the opening paragraph is scarcely less negative in its vocabulary ('becalmed … amputated … lost', p. 96) than the description of the Fertilizing Room which in Chapter 1 introduced us to the World State.

Bernard claims to be impressed by the maternal experience of childbirth and breast-feeding but, even if we agree with these views which he advances largely in order to provoke Lenina, as outsiders we cannot help looking critically at other features of the Indians' culture. Their method of dealing with ageing is not necessarily more attractive than the World State's and few will experience enthusiasm for the fertility ritual which they enact to placate 'Pookong and Jesus'. The Indians, unable to control or insulate themselves from nature, instead confront its dangers irrationally through rituals, handling snakes and beating a human sacrifice until he falls. As with the Solidarity Service, we can detect some remnants of Christianity in the ceremony, or perhaps the presence of ideas which unite all religions (a notion Huxley was later to explore in his book *The Perennial Philosophy*), with a young man scourged like Jesus before the crucifixion, then sacrificed for the benefit of others, with three women later coming to care for his body. It is unclear whether the victim is injured or actually dead, and for a moment, as we enter into the shocked feelings of the visitors, the book seems to be losing its flippantly satirical tone. Then John appears, with his preposterous mix of upper-class and Shakespearean English, to supply comic relief. This comedy of the incongruous continues with the visit to his mother, Linda, who looks like a savage but embraces the horrified Lenina as a fellow citizen, immersing her in a rambling monologue on the problems of being caught between two worlds with violently conflicting customs.

> **CONTEXT**
>
> Huxley's *The Perennial Philosophy* (1946) is an anthology of spiritual writing from many cultures which tries to establish 'the highest common factor of all the higher religions'.

GLOSSARY

100	ophthalmia	inflammation of the eye
104	damned spot	from *Macbeth* V.1.35
105	The multitudinous seas incarnadine	from *Macbeth* II.2.59
	disliked me for my complexion	echoes *The Merchant of Venice* II.1.1
108	*mescal ... peyotl*	hallucogenic drugs made from the peyote cactus
	Streptocock-Gee to Banbury T	an adaptation of the nursery rhyme 'Ride a cock-horse to Banbury Cross / To see a fine lady upon a white horse.' Streptococcus is a bacterium which produces infections
109	embryopoison	alcohol

CHAPTER 8

- Prompted by Bernard, John recalls his childhood.
- Both men recognise that they are outsiders in their societies.
- John is delighted when Bernard offers to take him and Linda back to London.

Bernard asks John about his childhood. John remembers how his mother's lovers came between him and her, and how her promiscuous sexual behaviour led women from the village to beat her and children to stone him. He always enjoyed hearing about the world from which Linda came, the Other Place, and he mixed it in his daydreams with the mythology of the village, itself a mixture of paganism and Christianity. Rejected by those around him, John found solace in a copy of Shakespeare's works which had been discovered by his mother's boyfriend, Popé, and, partly inspired by Hamlet's example, he tried unsuccessfully to stab Popé to death. He also found consolation in traditional clay-modelling. However, John remained unaccepted and was not allowed to take part in the initiation ceremony which would have permitted him to become a man of the tribe. In defiance, John devised and carried out his own initiation rites, torturing himself by starvation and standing in the sun in a crucifix pose.

CONTEXT

Shakespeare's play *The Tempest* (1610/11) tells of a duke with magical powers who is exiled with his daughter on a remote island, and what happens when the very people who betrayed him are then shipwrecked there.

After hearing all this, Bernard invites John to return to London with him. When John asks if Linda can come too, Bernard is at first reluctant, then realises that she may be a valuable asset in his conflict with the Director. Excited by the prospect of entering the world of his daydreams, John quotes Miranda's words from Shakespeare's play *The Tempest*: 'O brave new world that has such people in it' (p. 126).

COMMENTARY

When Bernard invites John to tell him about his life, we might expect to hear his account. Instead, most of the chapter uses **free indirect discourse** to take us into John's experiences, placing us directly into his point of view and moving us economically through the key episodes of his formative experience. John's childhood is rendered almost as a **stream of consciousness**, with the reader able to 'read between the lines' and infer more than John himself as a child can realise. We find ourselves sympathising with him as he is dominated by Linda's chief lover Popé, is unable to protect her from the women who beat her for her promiscuity, and is rejected at least some of the time by Linda herself. John's childhood is the reverse of that experienced by the citizens of the World State. Where their experiences are controlled and identical, his are random and unique. Neither is satisfactory.

John's discovery of Shakespeare helps give shape to his experiences, as he perceives his situation to be similar to that of *Hamlet* in relation to Gertrude and Claudius. However, we should not assume, as some critics have done, that his knowledge of Shakespeare is an entirely good thing. While the plays help to articulate John's feelings and offer him alternative ways of thinking, they also offer him some unwise role models. *Hamlet* encourages him to try to murder Popé; *Othello* later leads him to attack Lenina.

His isolation and Shakespeare-fostered sensitivity make John more thoughtful than his peers, and these qualities appeal to Bernard, who understands at least some of his sense of rejection by society. We resent Bernard's sense of superiority and feel for John, yet we agree that Bernard really does know better than John when the latter quotes Miranda's words from *The Tempest*, spoken when, having grown up on a remote island, she meets some of the first men other than her father that she has ever seen. John has not perceived Shakespeare's **irony** in this passage. (Again, simply reading Shakespeare is not enough. The reader needs to draw upon the responses of others in order to understand fully.) Miranda is naive and does not realise that few of the men she sees are other than ordinary, nor that some of them are thoroughly wicked. We have no doubt that John too faces disillusion.

CONTEXT

In Shakespeare's play *Hamlet* (1600/1), Hamlet, the Prince of Denmark, is disgusted when shortly after his father's death his mother marries his father's brother, Claudius. He then learns from his father's ghost that Claudius was his murderer. Hamlet's quest for revenge culminates in the destruction of the entire royal family.

GLOSSARY

111	'Bye, Baby Banting' an adaptation of the nursery rhyme 'Bye, baby bunting, / Daddy's gone a-hunting'
115	little animals lice
119	'Nay, but to live … sty' from *Hamlet* III.4.91–4
	A man can smile and smile and be a villain from *Hamlet* I.5.108
	Remorseless, treacherous, lecherous, kindless villain from *Hamlet* II.2.581
120	When he is drunk asleep … from *Hamlet* III.3.89–90
123	kiva underground chamber used for religious rites
124	Tomorrow and tomorrow and tomorrow from *Macbeth* V.5.19
126	How many goodly creatures … O brave new world from *The Tempest* V.1.181–4 ('brave' here means 'splendid')

CHAPTER 9

- Lenina takes refuge in a drugged sleep and Bernard obtains permission to bring John and Linda to London.
- Meanwhile, John sneaks into the outsiders' room.

After her stressful day in the Reservation, Lenina recuperates by taking enough *soma* to make her sleep for at least eighteen hours. Bernard uses this time to fly by helicopter to Santa Fé, where he can make a telephone call to the World Controller, asking permission to bring John and Linda to London. Mond agrees. John, meanwhile, fearing the visitors have left, breaks into the house where Bernard and Lenina have been staying. He investigates Lenina's belongings and feels lust for her, before the sound of Bernard's helicopter returning startles him into leaving.

COMMENTARY

Bernard's phone call moves the plot forward a step, but the main purpose of this chapter is to develop and emphasise John's character further. In creeping into Lenina's bedroom, then running off when Bernard returns, he is re-enacting his relationship with Linda and Popé, longing for a woman he believes to be unattainable and defeated by an older male figure who already possesses her. Here Huxley is evoking the psychologist Freud's concept of the Oedipus complex: that the growth of a man's sexuality involves a period in childhood when he experiences a passionate desire for his mother and a corresponding hatred and fear of his father, and that the failure to outgrow these feelings is the source of many later mental and behavioural problems. Freud thought that this psychological situation was the origin of the stories of Oedipus and Hamlet. Huxley, however, took a sceptical view of Freud's ideas and intended John's behaviour to be an amusing parody of them rather than a testimony to Freud's insights. John projects on to Lenina the ideal of womanhood which he has taken from his rather superficial reading of Shakespeare, failing to see that her way of life is the same promiscuous one as Linda's.

 CHECK THE BOOK

Freud: A Very Short Introduction by Anthony Storr (1989) explains Freud's theories. There is a sceptical assessment in Richard Webster's *Why Freud Was Wrong: Sin, Science and Psychoanalysis* (1995).

John's behaviour diminishes him further in the eyes of the reader. John has already failed to notice Lenina's disgust at Linda or Bernard's shudder at his scar. Added to this naive lack of perception, we now see his lack of self-control (when he thinks they may have gone back without him, he cries), his sexual timidity and his fetishistic handling of Lenina's clothing. All these suggest that he is trapped in the role of victim sketched in the previous chapter. Like Bernard's childishness, the defects in his character tend later in the book to undermine the power of his criticisms of the World State.

GLOSSARY

127	Agaves cactus plants
129	zippi-camiknicks camiknickers are a form of female underwear consisting of a light part to cover the top half of the body, connected to a pair of knickers, in this case with a zip fastener
130	'Her eyes, her hair, her cheek …' from *Troilus and Cressida* I.1.54–8
	'Flies … On the white wonder …' echoes *Romeo and Juliet* III.3.35–9
131	Dare to profane with his unworthiest hand echoes *Romeo and Juliet* I.5.93

CONTEXT

Shakespeare's play *Romeo and Juliet* (1594/5) tells of the doomed love between two young people who come from families that are feuding with each other.

CHAPTER 10

- The Director attempts to dismiss Bernard publicly from his post.
- The Director is himself humiliated when Bernard produces his former lover and biological child.

At the Central London Hatchery, the Director explains to Henry Foster that he will mark Bernard's return by making a public example of him. When Bernard arrives, the Director denounces him and tries to dismiss him from his post. Bernard responds, however, by bringing Linda into the room. The workers are shocked by her appearance and disgusted when she announces that the Director had once made her pregnant. When John arrives and greets the Director as his father, the onlookers find the situation so gross and absurd that they burst into near-hysterical laughter, and the Director is forced to flee in humiliation.

CHECK THE BOOK

In *Crome Yellow*, a satirical novel written by Huxley in 1921, a character called Scogan sketches the ideas about the future later developed in *Brave New World*.

COMMENTARY

The story returns to the urban and artificial world, its mechanical conformity stressed by the opening **image** of four thousand synchronised clocks, which is repeated from Chapter 3. The Director intends to punish Bernard for his failure to conform, but **ironically** it is he who is punished for deviance. This dramatic reversal, with the reader knowing more than the characters and waiting in suspense for the likely outcome, is a classic comic situation, and Huxley makes the most of it. The Director is so insufferably malicious and pompous that we are delighted when his plan backfires. (Here Huxley has to explain the exact associations of the word 'father' for the onlookers so that we understand the 'punchline', and he makes a skilful use of **parenthesis** to insert the explanation without disturbing the flow of the narrative.) The Director is forced to flee in humiliation, putting Bernard and, with him, John into a new position of strength. However, their victory is a very limited one. Conformity itself is not challenged. The Centre workers regard Linda with derision and are 'almost hysterical' (p. 137) at the idea of John seeking his father.

GLOSSARY	
132	**Bloomsbury** district containing the British Museum and the University of London, and associated in Huxley's day with the cultured authors and artists of the 'Bloomsbury Group'
133	**It is better that one should suffer than that many should be corrupted** compare John 18:14: 'it was expedient that one man should die for the people'

CHAPTER 11

- As John explores modern civilisation, he is more and more repelled by what he sees.
- Lenina takes him to watch a feely, assuming that it will arouse him, and is disappointed when he does not stay the night with her.

Linda's response to her homecoming is to take so much *soma* that she will die within two months. John tries to object to this but is overruled. He, in contrast, is keen to investigate the new society and, since his encounter with the Director has made him the object of public curiosity, he is welcomed everywhere. Bernard takes full advantage of his role as the Savage's guardian to meet as many dignitaries and have as many women as possible. However, Bernard continues to take a critical view of society and expresses his opinions in his reports on the Savage to the World Controller. John finds what he sees in the brave new world more and more repulsive. He is physically sick at the sight of groups of identical workers, offended when the students of Eton College laugh at a film of primitive customs, and shocked by a pornographic feely, which he attends with Lenina. Lenina hopes that he will spend the night at her apartment, but John flees from her. While she takes *soma* to console herself, he goes to his hidden copy of Shakespeare and reads *Othello*.

> **CONTEXT**
>
> Huxley was a pupil at Eton from 1908 to 1911 and a teacher there from 1917 to 1919. One of the pupils to whom he taught French, while struggling to control the class due to his poor eyesight, was George Orwell, later the author of *Nineteen Eighty-Four*.

COMMENTARY

At this point in the book the anti-**utopian** forces seem to be in the ascendant, with John and Bernard transformed from rejects into celebrities whom everyone wants to meet. However, they are not respected as critics of society, only enjoyed as the latest sensation, a freak and his keeper. Bernard enjoys his celebrity status so much that he embraces conformity and fails to build on his friendship with Helmholtz, from whom indeed he makes a point of distancing himself. By showing us Bernard's behaviour through the eyes, first of Helmholtz, then of Mond, Huxley ensures that we see him in a critical perspective.

Bernard writes what is largely a pro-society commentary on John's behaviour for the World Controller, assuming he will be enlightened by it. In fact Mond finds Bernard's attitude patronising and, although amused, feels disposed to punish him. It is John who maintains a critical view of 'civilisation' for us and, while we may find ourselves agreeing with many of his reactions, admiring him for his refusal to take *soma* and sympathising when he vomits at the sight of a factory full of mass-produced Deltas and Gammas, it is equally likely that we will find some of his quotations from Shakespeare smug and his reaction to Lenina's advances somewhat priggish. John's recourse to *Othello* at the end of the chapter is less an affirmation of culture over vulgarity than a retreat from experience into the distancing world of the book, and when we recall Othello's murder of Desdemona because he believed that she was not chaste, it seems an ominous development.

CONTEXT

In Shakespeare's *Othello* (1602–4), General Othello, a Moor in the army of Venice (and so, like John, an outsider) falls in love with the daughter of a senator, Desdemona. They elope together but Othello's ensign, Iago, falsely persuades him that she is having an affair and Othello strangles her, then, realising his folly, kills himself.

GLOSSARY

139	Eternity was in our lips and eyes from *Antony and Cleopatra* I.3.35
142	Dravidian of southern Indian or Sri Lankan origin
	Ariel could put a girdle round the earth in forty minutes either John or Huxley is confusing Ariel in *The Tempest* with Robin Goodfellow, the Puck, in *A Midsummer Night's Dream* II.1.175–6
144	cold-pressing flattening metal without first heating it
	chucking and turning machines lathes
	prognathous jutting
145	Eton the well-known public school at which Huxley himself was a pupil from 1908 to 1911 and a teacher from 1917 to 1919
	Lupton's Tower a sixteenth-century structure at Eton; here rebuilt into a skyscraper
	statue of Our Ford replacing the bronze statue of Henry VI, the school's founder
	Dr Gaffney a Dr Gaffney was the school clerk at Eton until his retirement in 1910
	Miss Keate the name recalls John Keate, reforming headmaster of Eton 1809–34
146	elementary relativity an introduction to Einstein's work on physics

148   the Savoy a famous London hotel

those caskets a reference to Acts I and II of *The Merchant of Venice*. Suitors for Portia could not marry her unless they chose the correct casket from the three they were offered. The two made of gold and silver did not deliver true happiness. Only the man who risked choosing the lead casket ('Who chooseth me must give and hazard all he hath', II.7.16) could win what he desired

149   the Young Women's Fordian Association the name recalls the Young Women's Christian Association, founded in 1855

Feelytone News Movietone News supplied newsreels to cinemas from June 1929

the Ford Chief-Justice the Lord Chief Justice is the second most important judge in the English legal system

the Arch-Community-Songster of Canterbury the Archbishop of Canterbury is the leader of the Church of England

the Bank of Europe no such institution existed in Huxley's day, but a European Investment Bank was set up in 1958, and in 1999 a European Central Bank was created in order to oversee the single European currency

150   Capriccio a short, lively piece of music; here, a sequence of smells

151   Gaspard Foster ... Lucrezia Ajugari Kaspar Förster was a seventeenth-century singer, famed for his low notes; Lucrezia Agujari (the correct spelling) was an eighteenth-century singer famed for her high notes

Three Weeks in a Helicopter the title recalls Elinor Glyn's *Three Weeks*, a romantic novel of 1907, notorious in its day for erotic scenes on a tiger-skin rug

QUESTION

Do you think it is necessary to have an understanding of the historical background of *Brave New World* in order to appreciate it as a work of literature?

CHAPTER 12

- Disgusted by what he has seen of modern society, John refuses to attend a party Bernard is holding in his honour.
- The distinguished guests depart in a hostile mood, shattering Bernard's new self-confidence.

- Elsewhere, the World Controller is banning a mathematical study of biology because it calls into question society's assumptions about the purpose of life.
- Bernard introduces John to Helmholtz, who has recently been threatened with dismissal from his job for writing poetry.
- John shows Helmholtz the writings of Shakespeare.

Bernard has invited a number of distinguished people to a party so that they can meet John. However, John, disgusted by what he has seen of their world, refuses to leave his room and remains inside, reading *Romeo and Juliet*. The guests are furious with Bernard and leave early, shattering his newly found self-confidence. In particular, the Arch-Community-Songster of Canterbury lectures him to mend his ways, before leaving in the company of Lenina.

Elsewhere, the World Controller is banning a mathematical study of biology because it calls into question society's assumption that the aim of life is simply to be happy. If some of the more intelligent members of society were to read this paper and begin to think that the goal of life was to expand human awareness, social stability might be threatened – even though, as the Controller admits to himself, it might be true.

CONTEXT

Huxley himself began his writing career with four books of poetry: *The Burning Wheel* (1916), *Jonah* (1917), *The Defeat of Youth* (1918) and *Leda* (1920)

Bernard, depressed again after his failed party, tells Helmholtz his troubles and finds that his friend has been threatened with dismissal for writing verses about being alone, and using them in one of his lectures on advertising technique. When Bernard introduces the Savage to Helmholtz, John impresses him by quoting from Shakespeare. Shakespeare's plays seem to Helmholtz to be comically old-fashioned in their attitudes, but he recognises that it was precisely the 'madness and violence' (p. 168) of human experience in the past that enabled the writer to express emotions so powerfully.

COMMENTARY

The chapter opens with a passage consisting largely of dialogue between Bernard and John through a closed door. John's refusal to leave his room ensures Bernard's humiliation in the rest of the chapter. Having eagerly seized the fruits of conformity, Bernard is now vulnerable to their loss. Our sympathy for him is tempered, however, because it was his own vanity that placed him in a position where these pompous, shallow people could sneer at him, and because he still fails to learn from his plight, merely consoling himself using the standard World State method, a dose of *soma*.

As in Chapter 11, we cut away briefly to Mond, not this time to hear his view of Bernard's ideas, but to see him censoring a biology research paper. This not only gives variety to the chapter, but also establishes Mond as a character who can exercise control over the lives of anyone he wishes and so prepares us for his later intervention in Chapter 16. Mond's thoughts clarify for us the fundamental assumption of the World State, that the purpose of life is simply 'the maintenance of well-being' and not, as Huxley implies it should or could be, the 'intensification and refining of consciousness' (p. 161). When John introduces Shakespeare's writings to Helmholtz, only to find that although he appreciates them he cannot take them seriously, we see that the Controllers have cut humanity off from the past to such an extent that new growth may be impossible.

GLOSSARY		
159	**Diocesan Singery**	the brave new world's equivalent to the main church of a district
160	**St Helena**	the South Atlantic island to which the British exiled Napoleon in 1815 after the Battle of Waterloo
161	**'O, she doth teach …'**	from *Romeo and Juliet* I.5.44–7
164	**'Lips and, ah, posteriors'**	recalls the last line of Gerard Manley Hopkins's poem 'God's Grandeur', which speaks of the Holy Ghost 'with ah! bright wings'
165	**'Let the bird of loudest lay …'**	the poem is Shakespeare's 'The Phoenix and the Turtle'
167	**'Is there no pity …'**	from *Romeo and Juliet* III.5.196–201

CONTEXT

Gerard Manley Hopkins (1844–89), a Catholic priest, was the author of powerful, innovative poems which celebrated God's presence in nature and grappled with spiritual torments. The language of his poems was too experimental for his own era and they were not published until almost thirty years after his death.

CHAPTER 13

CHECK THE FILM

This scene is left out of Michael R. Joyce's 1998 film adaptation of *Brave New World*. Why do you think it was excluded?

- Lenina has fallen in love with John. She visits him to tell him so.
- When he admits to his feelings for her, she tries to make love to him but, disgusted by her behaviour, he responds by assaulting her.
- John then receives a telephone message that Linda is dying and hurries off to see her.

Lenina has become so in love with the unattainable John that she quarrels with Henry and makes a mistake in her work in the Embryo Store. Fanny advises her to fortify her courage with *soma* and make John have sex with her. Lenina goes to him as advised and he expresses both his admiration for her and his frustration at not knowing how to court her and propose marriage. Lenina dismisses these ideas, removes her clothes and embraces him. However, John is disgusted by her forward actions and responds by attacking her, forcing her to take refuge in the bathroom. While she is there, a message comes by telephone, telling John that his mother Linda is dying. He hurries off to be at her deathbed, allowing Lenina to escape.

COMMENTARY

The contrast between Lenina and Henry at the opening of the chapter suggests that she is no longer a model citizen of the World State, promiscuous and easy-going like him, but has developed an old-fashioned, obsessive love for John. If we are willing to regard love as a kind of infection, then Henry's anxiety that she may have caught one of the few remaining infectious diseases is true. Paradoxically, it is John's refusal to have sex with her that makes him special and causes her to want him so much. Lenina and John have grown up in such different worlds, however, that they prove incapable of developing their feelings for each other in a mutually intelligible and acceptable way. Lenina's unsuccessful visit to him should be one of the saddest episodes in the book – changing, when John assaults her, to an alarming one – but, in keeping with his preference for 'stereoscopic' **characterisation**, Huxley contrives to make it humorous (see **Critical approaches**, on **Narrative technique and structure**). Perhaps the idea of a woman wooing a man is not so amusing today as it might have been in the 1920s, but Lenina's aggressive approach, embracing him, then beginning to strip off her clothes, while he, in his turn, responds with terror and flight, is still bound to strike most readers as hilarious. Neither character's behaviour can be taken seriously. From their crossed-purpose conversation, we proceed rapidly to farce, as John switches from fear to aggression, assaulting Lenina so that, with a culminating slap across the bottom, she is forced to hide naked in the bathroom till he has gone. The telephone call which brings news of Linda's decline restores some element of seriousness, balanced in its turn by Lenina's comically nervous escape.

GLOSSARY

169	jim-jams nervous agitation
	V.P.S. Violent Passion Surrogate (the term is explained at the end of Chapter 17)
170	trypanosomiasis sleeping sickness
171	Y.W.F.A. Young Women's Fordian Association
172	'Admired Lenina ...' adapted from *The Tempest* III.1.37–48
173	'There be some sports are painful ...' from *The Tempest* III.1.1–2
174	Outliving beauty's outward ... from *Troilus and Cressida* III.2.162–3
	'If thou dost break her virgin knot ...' from *The Tempest* IV.1.15–17
	'The murkiest den ...' from *The Tempest* IV.1.25–8
175	too, too solid certainty recalls *Hamlet* I.2.129
	'For those milk paps ...' from *Timon of Athens* IV.3.116–7
	'The strongest oaths ...' from *The Tempest* IV.1.52–4
176	'Whore! Impudent strumpet!' from *Othello* IV.2.81–6
177	'The wren goes to't ...' from *King Lear* IV.6.112–3
178	'O thou weed ...' echoes *Othello* IV.2.67–77
	The devil Luxury ... from *Troilus and Cressida* V.2.55–6. Luxury: lechery.

continued

CONTEXT

Shakespeare's play *Troilus and Cressida* (1601) tells of the doomed love of two people from opposite sides in the Trojan War. Cressida betrays Troilus by allowing herself to becomes Diomedes' mistress.

178	potato finger finger arousing lust (potatoes were thought to have aphrodisiac power)
179	**If I do not usurp myself, I am** from *Twelfth Night* I.5.186
	Park Lane a road in London's affluent Mayfair

CHAPTER 14

- John is distraught beside Linda's deathbed.
- No one can understand his grief as no one else has a close bond to any other human being.
- The children brought to the scene for 'death conditioning' have no sympathy and even Linda whispers only of Popé when John speaks to her. Ironically, the furious shaking of her with which he responds to this seems to hasten her death.

CONTEXT
Huxley was devastated by the death of his own mother when he was fourteen.

John finds Linda in a drugged stupor at the Park Lane Hospital for the Dying. The nurse who leads him to her cannot understand why John is so upset, and regards it as normal to bring eight-year-olds to the scene for 'death-conditioning'. John is aghast at the sight of a large number of identical boys behaving disrespectfully and drives them away. He then tries to remember good moments with his mother, but can only think of past misery and jealousy, while Linda herself whispers of her love for Popé, rejecting John once again. John shakes her in an attempt to get her attention, but her breathing fails and she dies, leaving him fearing that he may have killed her. The nurse uses cakes to distract the attention of the children from John's grief, so that the children will not be influenced by his behaviour and come to think of an individual's death as a terrible loss. When some of the children return to look at Linda's corpse, John knocks one of them down, then walks away.

COMMENTARY

The first paragraph of this chapter recalls the opening of the novel. There we were disorientated by a description of a 'squat' thirty-four-storey building. Here we read of a sixty-storey tower which is the colour of primroses and is the base for hearses which take the form of gaily coloured helicopters. Clearly the World State's view of death is very different from ours, or the savages'. The approach purports to be a rational acceptance of death's inevitability, but in fact it is a systematic denial of the experience. Linda is too drugged to know what is happening to her (her 'expression of imbecile happiness', p. 181, epitomises the society to which she has returned), while easy-listening music, perfumes and continuous television dispel any sense that something serious and significant is taking place. To John's disgust, children are even brought to the ward to be desensitised, so that they regard the end of a unique human being as a trivial matter.

However, John's own response is also inappropriate: a self-deceivingly sentimental one in which he tries to fabricate the happy memories he lacks, then an aggressive demand for recognition which places his own needs above those of the dying woman. Once more a terrible moment is reduced to farce, as John's attempt to get through to Linda seems to result in her death, and the moment of her extinction is trivialised, not only by the apparatus of the World State, but also by John's own slapstick antics, racing up and down the ward calling for help and knocking down an unsympathetic child. One part of us may feel that John's behaviour is contemptible, even amusing. Another part must recognise that at this point John feels totally rejected and is at the point of breakdown. Bernard has tried to use him, Helmholtz has laughed at his Shakespeare plays, Lenina has not lived up to his ideal of womanhood and even his mother has rejected him with her dying breath.

> **CONTEXT**
>
> Dickens's novel *Hard Times* attacks utilitarianism, the belief that society should be organised rationally in order to promote the happiness of the majority, a programme which he judged to be dangerously simplistic. The story begins in a school where the children memorise lists of facts with no understanding of what they mean, and are discouraged from taking any interest in the emotions or the imagination.

> **GLOSSARY**
>
> | 181–2 | Super-Vox-Wurlitzeriana the Wurlitzer organ supplied musical interludes in many cinemas of the 1930s |
> |---|---|
> | 187 | Bed 20 the term recalls Charles Dickens's novel *Hard Times* (1854), where, in the dehumanised educational system of Mr Gradgrind, Sissy Jupe is reduced to 'Girl Number 20' |

CHAPTER 15

- John tries to free the Hospital's menial workers from their social conditioning by preventing the distribution of *soma* to them, throwing their pills out of the window.
- Helmholtz and Bernard try to rescue him from the angry mob.
- All three are saved when the police arrive and suppress the riot.

John finds himself in the midst of the one hundred and sixty-two Deltas who carry out the menial work at the Hospital and who are queuing to receive their daily allowance of *soma*. He is repelled by their uniform appearance and by their dependency on the drug, and decides to set them free from it by flinging the tablet boxes out of the window. Bernard and Helmholtz arrive in time to witness this scene. Helmholtz tries to save John from the angry mob, while Bernard stands irresolutely to one side. The police arrive and suppress the riot by firing water pistols filled with anaesthetic and playing a record of soothing music and speech. The Deltas are given a fresh supply of *soma*. John, Helmholtz and Bernard are arrested.

COMMENTARY

This is the sole episode in the book where a revolt is attempted against the World State and, characteristically, it is less a display of revolutionary heroism than a piece of farcical slapstick. Observing the distribution of *soma* from John's point of view, we share his anger, but his plan of action seems as sentimental and self-deceiving as his response to the dying Linda. How will depriving the workers of their *soma* suddenly render the world 'beautiful' (p. 192)? A reader in 1932 would probably be reminded of Prohibition, the banning of alcohol in the USA from 1920 to 1933, which was sometimes called the 'noble experiment'. The ban was intended to free people from addiction and crime, but in practice it caused widespread law-breaking and enriched the gangsters who took over the trade. John's idealism is to be similarly unsuccessful.

The battle between John and Helmholtz, on the one hand, and the Deltas, on the other, with the police intervening to restore order

CHECK THE FILM

In Michael R. Joyce's 1998 film adaptation of *Brave New World*, there are repeated failures of conditioning, suggesting much more strongly than in Huxley's book that human nature may be resistant to technological shaping.

using *soma*-vapour water pistols, is a **burlesque** one, more like a game than a fight where someone might be lastingly hurt, and the only note of seriousness comes at the end when, in a rare moment of commitment, Bernard refuses to deny that he is a friend of John and Helmholtz and is taken prisoner with them.

If the World State is so stable, why, it might be asked, are there riot police ready for rapid intervention? While the authorities are clearly capable of maintaining order, here is another indication that this brave new world is not so 'perfect' as its leaders claim.

GLOSSARY

190	dolichocephalic long-headed
192	Lend me your ears … from *Julius Caesar* III.2.73
194	Mewling and puking from *As You Like It* II.7.144

CHAPTER 16

- The three captives are taken to the Controller's study, where he reiterates the need for stability.
- Stability can be achieved only if society is organised as at present, even if the limits this imposes on individual development include abolishing the pursuit of serious art and science.
- Bernard and Helmholtz are banished to remote islands.

Bernard, Helmholtz and John are taken to the study of the Controller. Mond reveals that he knows the works of Shakespeare, but insists that his plays must not be made available to others. They are based on change and passion, experiences which modern society has abolished. When asked by John why science cannot be used to produce only intelligent and fit people, he explains that this was tried once in Cyprus, but the Alphas soon became discontented and civil war broke out. Nor would it be constructive to reduce the working hours of the lower castes with labour-saving processes, since more leisure would make them unhappy. Like art, science is

CONTEXT

The islands to which the dissidents are banished seem to derive from Chapter 5 of H.G. Wells's *A Modern Utopia* (1905), 'Failure in a Modern Utopia'. The islands would be off normal sea routes and arrangements would be made to prevent those sent there from having any children who might inherit their antisocial attitudes.

a potentially subversive force. In his youth Mond himself was a scientist who pursued unorthodox ideas and risked banishment to an island but, when offered the choice, he preferred to join the Controllers' Council and keep the world a stable place. Bernard and Helmholtz will, however, be sent to islands where they can mingle with other independent-minded people. Bernard is horrified at this prospect, but Helmholtz looks forward to writing in the stormy climate of the Falklands.

COMMENTARY

QUESTION

Looking back on *Brave New World* many years later, Huxley wrote: 'the most serious defect in the story' is that the 'Savage is offered only two alternatives, an insane life in Utopia, or the life of a primitive in an Indian village' (Foreword, pp. i–ii). Do you agree that the novel would be more effective if it contained more or better 'alternatives'?

Mond is the most authoritative and knowledgeable character in *Brave New World*. If the book was simply a political-philosophical essay in fictional form, then his account of why the world is as it is, and the ensuing discussion about whether it should be changed, would form its conclusion. With his look of 'good-humoured intelligence' (p. 199), Mond declines to act as a storybook villain, but puts forward his views with charm and logic, addressing the reader as much as his fellow characters. If people are to be happy, then they need to live in a stable, supportive environment. High art and scientific research, which explore beauty and truth, are forces of disruption. They must therefore be replaced by light entertainment and applied science. In making this point, Mond does not deny the quality of Shakespeare's work, but he asserts other priorities above its appreciation. Authentic, fully living people do still exist in the World State, but they are two very small minorities, the exiles on the islands and the World Controllers. When Bernard and Helmholtz depart to join the former, the spokesman of the World State, Mond, and his most committed critic, John, are left to conclude the debate.

GLOSSARY

198	**at Detroit** centre of the American motor industry, the city where Henry Ford lived and worked
	the Society for the Propagation of Fordian Knowledge the name echoes the Society for the Propagation of Christian Knowledge, founded in 1698
199	**Sometimes a thousand twangling instruments ...** from *The Tempest* III.2.137–8

200	**Goats and monkeys!** from *Othello* III.3.403
201	**told by an idiot** from *Macbeth* V.5.27
205	**Corn Dances** ritual dances to encourage the growth of the crops
206	**scullion** dishwasher, kitchen assistant
207	**the primitive matriarchies** societies ruled by women, which existed before male-dominated societies (it is no longer believed that these existed)
209	**The Marquesas ... Samoa** islands in the South Pacific which had previously served as retreats for nineteenth-century artists, the painter Paul Gauguin living in the former, the writer Robert Louis Stevenson in the latter

CHAPTER 17

- When Helmholtz and Bernard have gone, John and the Controller discuss God.
- Mond thinks that God may exist, but argues that, even if He does, society no longer has need of Him.
- John protests that he does not want to live by the rules of such a society. He would rather have God, freedom and poetry, even if the cost for himself is insecurity and pain.

CHECK THE BOOK

Fyodor Dostoevsky's chapter 'The Grand Inquisitor' in his novel *The Brothers Karamazov* (1880) is sometimes said to be a model for Chapters 16 and 17 of *Brave New World*. (See **Intertextuality**.)

Mond points out that, along with serious art and science, society has had to abandon God. He is interested in this subject and keeps sacred texts and books about religion (which he calls 'pornographic', p. 210) securely hidden in a safe. Reading from them, he makes the point that traditionally people turn to religion as they grow older, but now that people retain youth and prosperity until the point of death, they have no need for religion. There may well be a God, but, if so, He is no longer relevant. John replies that modern people are degraded by their way of life and therefore they are being punished by God for their wickedness, even though they do not know it. Mond remains certain that modern society has brought everyone the happiness they need, with a monthly Violent

Passion Surrogate chemically compensating them for any lack of danger and uncertainty. John rejects this solution. He would rather have God, freedom and poetry, even at the cost of insecurity and pain.

COMMENTARY

> **CONTEXT**
>
> In a 1961 interview Huxley summed up the 'message' of the book simply as 'This is possible: for heaven's sake, be careful about it.'

One of the most thought-provoking chapters in the book, this is also perhaps one of the least satisfactory in its presentation of the issues it raises. The debate between the two men calls attention to the importance of religion, yet it does not establish at all clearly that the World State lacks religious awareness or that any particular religion should be introduced into it. Far from asserting that the loss of Christianity should be remedied, Huxley seems to enjoy making a travesty of Christianity through the sign of the T, the Arch-Community-Songster and so on. When Mond quotes from de Biran and Newman, the translations silently delete references to the fundamental Christian doctrines of the creation and redemption. To John, for whom Jesus and Pookong are equal deities, what is at stake is not the doctrines of Christianity or any other religion, but the mere recognition of the idea of God and of the sense of the sacred, yet we have seen that the World State does make some provision for these things through the Solidarity Service in Chapter 5. Perhaps the real issue is that the 'Greater Being' (Chapter 2, p. 72) invoked by the Solidarity Group is merely a symbol of their common humanity, not a deity separate from the human species which could offer them a purpose and value beyond themselves. Unfortunately, Huxley does not make this distinction clear, and when Mond puts it to the Savage that his complaints about the World State are essentially negative ones which boil down to a preference for pain, it is difficult not to conclude that he has the best of the argument. The conclusion is reinforced by John's frequently immature behaviour and his history of inflicting suffering upon himself due to psychological disturbance. Perhaps the force of the book is increased because none of the World State's critics is able to supply the reader with a convincing alternative ideal. To sum up, we may see some force in John's assertion that human beings need a transcendent set of values, but we are not given encouragement to accept the views of any particular religion. In the next chapter we see John praying to Awonawilona, Jesus, Pookong and the eagle.

GLOSSARY

210	*The Imitation of Christ* a book of religious reflections by Thomas à Kempis (1427)
	The Varieties of Religious Experience a study of religious experiences by the American psychologist William James (1902)
211	Cardinal Newman an influential Victorian churchman who left the Church of England to become a Roman Catholic in 1845. Mond quotes from an abridged version of the sixth sermon in Volume 5 of *Parochial and Plain Sermons*
	'I, Pandulph, of fair Milan cardinal' from *King John* III.1.138
	Maine de Biran a French philosopher and politician. Mond quotes from his *Journal*, 6 and 7 June 1818
	A man who dreams of fewer things than there are in heaven and earth a reference to *Hamlet* I.5.166–7
214	Bradley F. H. Bradley, an English philosopher who argued that all individuals are part of a greater whole
	King Lear the reference is to V.3.171–5
215	But value dwells not in particular will from *Troilus and Cressida* II.2.53–6
216	neurasthenia weakness of the nerves
217	what Othello said from *Othello* II.1.185–6
	Whether 'tis nobler in the mind … from *Hamlet* III.1.56–9
218	all that fortune, death and danger dare … from *Hamlet* IV.4.51–3
	adrenals glands producing adrenalin, which helps the body to respond when violent actions are needed

CONTEXT

William James's *The Varieties of Religious Experience* is a highly original work which examines religion, not in terms of whether it is true or false, but for its psychological effects on individual morale.

CHAPTER 18

- John withdraws from society and lives in an old air-lighthouse, trying to become holy.
- His practice of whipping himself as a punishment for his sins attracts press attention.

- At first he drives the reporters away, but a documentary film about him, made using long-distance cameras, draws a crowd of spectators, including Lenina and Henry.
- In an outburst of frustration, John goes berserk and beats Lenina, initiating an orgy of sex and violence.
- After he comes round and realises what he has done, John hangs himself.

John is so determined to reject modern 'civilisation' that he reverts to savage customs, making himself vomit in order to purify himself of its influence. When Bernard and Helmholtz depart for their respective islands, John seeks his own form of escape, living alone in an abandoned air-lighthouse, away from the main transport routes. Here he tries to become self-sufficient and at times does feel happy, but he can never forget his treatment of Linda or his lust for Lenina, which arouse feelings of deep guilt. He punishes himself by holding uncomfortable poses and by beating himself with a whip. This is seen by passers-by and soon journalists come to investigate. John responds to their questions by assaulting them and he is left alone for a while. Then a photographer uses telescopic lenses to film his self-flagellation and makes the spectacle into a 'feely'. On the afternoon of the film's release, a crowd of spectators arrive in helicopters to see John's behaviour for themselves, shouting at him to perform for them as though he were an animal in a circus. Lenina and Henry are among them and, although Lenina seems to have come out of love for him, John loses his self-control at the sight of her and attacks her with the whip. The other spectators mimic his behaviour, beating one another in an orgy of violence. When they have gone, John awakens from sleep and realises what he has done. When the next wave of sightseers arrive, they find that John has hanged himself.

CHECK THE FILM

In Michael R. Joyce's 1998 film adaptation of *Brave New World*, John dies accidentally, leaving Bernard and Lenina to discover love together. When she becomes pregnant, the couple escape to the 'savage' reservation to raise their child in freedom. Would you judge this ending to be better or worse than Huxley's? Why?

COMMENTARY

Given the scope of its themes, *Brave New World* is a book for which it cannot have been easy for Huxley to devise a conclusion. At the level of discussion, how is the debate about the good or evil of the World State to be resolved? The answer is that it cannot be resolved, or at least it cannot without reducing the book's power, and undermining its questioning character. The ending therefore needs to shift us away from the recent abstract discussions towards a symbolic event which can re-pose the questions with dramatic finality. At the same time, at the personal level, the book needs to resolve what is to become of John, who is not at home on the Reservation or in London.

Initially we are distanced from John by viewing his reversion to savage practices through the eyes of Helmholtz. Looking from this rational perspective, readers are unlikely to accept John's view that drinking a mustard solution in order to make himself throw up is a sensible answer to his problems. Helmholtz, Bernard and Mond are then withdrawn from the story.

When John (or the Savage, as he is now more often called – another distancing device) takes up residence in an abandoned air-lighthouse, we are told of the traffic accidents that had previously occurred in the vicinity, creating a suggestion of doom. John's self-punishment is a demeaning parody of the behaviour of religious hermits (a parallel might be made with Alfred Tennyson's comic poem of 1833, 'St Simeon Stylites'). In time, his comparatively natural, self-reliant lifestyle does begin to make him happy but, caught in a neurotic behaviour pattern, he feels guilty about this as well and so continues to beat himself, confusing integrity with self-punishment.

While the reader is bound to be appalled by John's self-destructive behaviour, it seems almost healthy when compared to the intrusive parasitism of the radio reporter who barges in on his privacy with a series of idiotic and insensitive questions and, worse still, the telescopic filming of John's suffering by a 'big-game photographer' (p. 230) which is rapidly released as a cinema entertainment. This piece of satire on journalistic invasion of privacy has certainly not lost its relevance over the decades. (For further discussion, see Text 3 of Extended commentaries.)

The concluding episodes of the story repeat the established pattern of treating events 'stereoscopically', as horror and as farce. John and the so-called civilised inhabitants of the brave new world surrender equally to the primitive motives of curiosity, lust, anger and guilt, leading to the beating of Lenina (which may, as one critic has assumed, end in rape), then the death of John. The treatment of these events may seem almost flippant, but since Huxley's brother Trevenen had hanged himself not far from the spot where John dies, we must assume that Huxley is serious in dramatising the total collapse of morale which occurs when someone fails to preserve deeply held values. ('Trev was not strong,' Huxley noted in a letter of 1914, 'but he had the courage to face life with ideals – and his ideals were too much for him'.) The directionless swinging of the feet of John's corpse, compared in a **simile** to 'two unhurried compass needles' (p. 237), makes the book's concluding point symbolically. Once the human race has taken total control of its own destiny, and abandoned belief in a God, it no longer has any outside reference point by which to judge its actions or steer its future course.

GLOSSARY

222	**between Puttenham and Elstead** the location is three miles west of Godalming in Surrey, where Huxley was born, an area in which he would have played as a child with his brother Trev, who hanged himself in 1914
	the guilty Claudius a reference to *Hamlet* III.3.36–98
224	**fire drill** a primitive wooden device for making a flame
	pan-glandular supplying nourishment to, or supplementing the work of, all the glands in the body
226	**nocked** notched at one end to take a bow string
228	**Primo Mellon** the name recalls General Miguel Primo de Rivera, dictator of Spain from 1923 to 1930; and Andrew Mellon, an American banker and industrialist
	Coccyx a polite term for the journalist's rear end
	The Fordian Science Monitor the title echoes the *Christian Science Monitor*, journal of the Christian Science religion founded in 1908 by Mary Baker Eddy
230	**Darwin Bonaparte** the name recalls Charles Darwin, whose *On the Origin of Species* (1859) changed humanity's view of its place in the universe; and Napoleon Bonaparte, French emperor (1804–15)
232	**all our yesterdays** from *Macbeth* V.5.22–3

CHECK THE BOOK

There is a helpful account of Darwin and Darwinism in *Darwin: A Very Short Introduction* by Jonathan Howard (1982).

232	A good kissing carrion from *Hamlet* II.2.182
	As flies to wanton boys … from *King Lear* IV.1.36–7
	ever-gentle gods from *King Lear* IV.6.217
	thy best of rest is sleep … from *Measure for Measure* III.1.17–19
	Perchance to dream … from *Hamlet* III.1.63–5
235	Fitchew polecat
	Fry, lechery, fry! from *Troilus and Cressida* V.2.56–7
236	incarnation of turpitude embodiment of depravity

QUESTION

What is the significance of the frequent quotations from Shakespeare in *Brave New World*?

EXTENDED COMMENTARIES

TEXT 1 – CHAPTER 2 (PP. 16–18)

The nurses stiffened to attention as the DHC came in.

'Set out the books,' he said curtly.

In silence the nurses obeyed his command. Between the rose bowls the books were duly set out – a row of nursery quartos opened invitingly each at some gaily coloured image of beast or fish or bird.

'Now bring in the children.'

They hurried out of the room and returned in a minute or two, each pushing a kind of tall dumb-waiter laden, on all its four wire-netted shelves, with eight-month-old babies, all exactly alike (a Bokanovsky Group, it was evident) and all (since their caste was Delta) dressed in khaki.

'Put them down on the floor.'

The infants were unloaded.

'Now turn them so that they can see the flowers and books.'

Turned, the babies at once fell silent, then began to crawl towards those clusters of sleek colours, those shapes so gay and brilliant on the white pages. As they approached, the sun came out of a momentary eclipse behind a cloud. The roses flamed up as though with a sudden passion from within; a new and profound significance seemed to suffuse the shining pages of the books. From the ranks of the crawling babies came little squeals of excitement, gurgles and twitterings of pleasure.

The Director rubbed his hands. 'Excellent!' he said. 'It might almost have been done on purpose.'

The swiftest crawlers were already at their goal. Small hands reached out uncertainly, touched, grasped, unpetalling the transfigured roses, crumpling the illuminated pages of the books. The Director waited until all were happily busy. Then, 'Watch carefully,' he said. And, lifting his hand, he gave the signal.

The Head Nurse, who was standing by a switchboard at the other end of the room, pressed down a little lever.

There was a violent explosion. Shriller and ever shriller, a siren shrieked. Alarm bells maddeningly sounded.

The children started, screamed; their faces were distorted with terror.

'And now,' the Director shouted (for the noise was deafening), 'now we proceed to rub in the lesson with a mild electric shock.'

He waved his hand again, and the Head Nurse pressed a second lever. The screaming of the babies suddenly changed its tone. There was something desperate, almost insane, about the sharp spasmodic yelps to which they now gave utterance. Their little bodies twitched and stiffened; their limbs moved jerkily as if to the tug of unseen wires.

'We can electrify that whole strip of floor,' bawled the Director in explanation. 'But that's enough,' he signalled to the nurse.

The explosions ceased, the bells stopped ringing, the shriek of the siren died down from tone to tone into silence. The swiftly twitching bodies relaxed, and what had become the sob and yelp of infant maniacs broadened out once more into a normal howl of ordinary terror.

'Offer them the flowers and the books again.'

CONTEXT

Although few people today support the behaviourist theory in its pure form, stimulus-response approaches are still valued in the form of 'behaviour therapy' to overcome phobias and other unwanted behaviours.

The nurses obeyed; but at the approach of the roses, at the mere sight of those gaily-coloured images of pussy and cock-a-doodle-doo and baa-baa black sheep, the infants shrank away in horror; the volume of their howling suddenly increased.

'Observe,' said the Director triumphantly, 'observe.'

This episode occurs at the start of Chapter 2 while the Director is showing his students around the Hatchery. His explanations to them also function as Huxley's explanations to us of how this brave new world works. Between the first two chapters, we may be surprised to note, we have missed learning about the Decanting Room which Foster was so keen for the students to see. The omission perhaps implies that Huxley's contemporaries might find the way the children are 'born' too horribly unnatural to contemplate. The only description we are ever given of the Decanting Room is at the start of Chapter 10, where we are simply told that it was where 'the newly-unbottled babes uttered their first yell of horror and amazement' (p. 132).

The present episode works on several levels. At the most fundamental, it is horrific. Despite the sinister care taken over their genetic inheritance and their conditioning in the bottle, the children still retain a delight in bright things and pictures of natural objects, but this enjoyment is now cruelly taken from them. In the course of the theft, they are transformed from autonomous individuals whose actions are described by a succession of lively verbs ('reached out ... touched, grasped, unpetalling ... crumpling') to victims whose actions are dictated by others like puppets', as a **simile** impresses upon us ('as if to the tug of unseen wires', p. 18). Repetition of the word 'little' emphasises the children's weakness and appeals to our protective instinct. They are helpless and innocent; the Director is a figure of unquestioned authority, supported by other adults and able to bring the latest technology to bear on his victims. When we read of how the babies are frightened and hurt, we can only conclude that a state which has to treat them in this way in order to ensure its own survival is sick and unnatural. Rather like the infants themselves, we are given an early shock here and no amount of cool reasoning later in the book can persuade us to change our minds.

CHECK THE BOOK

Matt Ridley in *Genome: Autobiography of a Species in 23 Chapters* (1999) calls *Brave New World* 'an environmental, not a genetic, hell'. Character is shaped by chemical adjustment in the 'womb', followed by conditioning and brainwashing, then maintained by stupefying drugs. According to Ridley, brainwashing would be unlikely to have the power to permanently change character that Huxley assumes.

On another level, we remain aware that we are being inducted into a **dystopian** novel and we enjoy incidentally the skill with which the author conveys the necessary information so dramatically and economically. Our main point of view is the students', but typically Huxley shifts the viewpoint frequently, taking us into an approximation of the babies' ('pussy and cock-a-doodle-doo') and into the viewpoint which an educated twentieth-century mind might have if it saw through their eyes ('The roses flamed up as though with a sudden passion from within', p. 17). This **image** helps to emphasise that the children will grow into adults incapable of an unpredictable passion or of being transfigured in any way.

CONTEXT

Brave New World was Huxley's fifth novel; his first, *Crome Yellow*, was published in 1921.

When the Director greets the convenient burst of sunshine by declaring, 'It might almost have been done on purpose', Huxley is indulging in a kind of joke between writer and reader. He has, of course, inserted the sunlight into the narrative on purpose, and so he is manipulating our reactions in a way not dissimilar to the way in which the Director manipulates the children's. The difference, as the remark makes clear, is that we know what is happening to us and appreciate the experience, and we are therefore collaborators, not victims.

In an odd way the **slapstick** quality of the trick that the Director plays on the babies adds a trace of humour to the passage. If we could physically see the children's distress, the experience would be harrowing, but the print medium distances us from it and turns the episode into a kind of practical joke. Overall the effect is unsettling, an example of what Huxley called his 'stereoscopic vision' (see **Narrative technique and structure**). From one angle we see how horrible the event is, but from another we watch it with a detachment which borders on amusement. Because there is no one in the story capable of registering the horror, the horror itself is sufficiently diminished for this to be possible, leaving us feeling slightly compromised perhaps by our enjoyment of what we are reading.

TEXT 2 – CHAPTER 3 (PP. 41–3)

'He's so ugly!' said Fanny.

'But I rather like his looks.'

'And then so *small*.' Fanny made a grimace; smallness was so horribly and typically low-caste.

'I think that's rather sweet,' said Lenina. 'One feels one would like to pet him. You know. Like a cat.'

Fanny was shocked. 'They say somebody made a mistake when he was still in the bottle – thought he was a Gamma and put alcohol into his blood-surrogate. That's why he's so stunted.'

'What nonsense!' Lenina was indignant.

'Sleep teaching was actually prohibited in England. There was something called liberalism. Parliament, if you know what that was, passed a law against it. The records survive. Speeches about liberty of the subject. Liberty to be inefficient and miserable. Freedom to be a round peg in a square hole.'

'But, my dear chap, you're welcome, I assure you. You're welcome.' Henry Foster patted the Assistant Predestinator on the shoulder. 'Everyone belongs to everyone else, after all.'

One hundred repetitions three nights a week for four years, thought Bernard Marx, who was a specialist on hypnopaedia. Sixty-two thousand four hundred repetitions make one truth. Idiots!

'Or the Caste System. Constantly proposed, constantly rejected. There was something called democracy. As though men were more than physico-chemically equal.'

'Well, all I can say is that I'm going to accept his invitation.'

Bernard hated them, hated them. But they were two, they were large, they were strong.

'The Nine Years' War began in A.F. 141.'

CONTEXT

A caste system is social system in which people have to remain in the social group into which they were born.

'Not even if it *were* true about the alcohol in his blood-surrogate.'

'Phosgene, chloropicrin, ethyl iodoacetate, diphenylcyanarsine, trichlormethyl chloroformate, dichlorethyl sulphide. Not to mention hydrocyanic acid.'

'Which I simply don't believe,' Lenina concluded.

'The noise of fourteen thousand aeroplanes advancing in open order. But in the Kurfurstendamm and the Eighth Arrondissement, the explosion of the anthrax bombs is hardly louder than the popping of a paper bag.'

'Because I *do* want to see a Savage Reservation.'

$CH_3C_6H_2(NO_2)_3 + Hg(CNO)_2$ = well, what? An enormous hole in the ground, a pile of masonry, some bits of flesh and mucus, a foot, with the boot still on it, flying through the air and landing, flop, in the middle of the geraniums – the scarlet ones; such a splendid show that summer!

'You're hopeless, Lenina, I give you up.'

'The Russian technique for infecting water supplies was particularly ingenious.'

Back turned to back, Fanny and Lenina continued their changing in silence.

'The Nine Years' War, the great Economic Collapse. There was a choice between World Control and destruction. Between stability and …'

'Fanny Crowne's a nice girl too,' said the Assistant Predestinator.

In the nurseries, the Elementary Class Consciousness lesson was over, the voices were adapting future demand to future industrial supply. 'I do love flying,' they whispered, 'I do love flying, I do love having new clothes, I do love …'

'Liberalism, of course, was dead of anthrax, but all the same you couldn't do things by force.'

CONTEXT

Liberalism, in the sense used here, is a belief in freedom for the individual and limited government. In the last hundred years or so, the recognition that some people are in a much better position to make use of their liberty than others has led liberals to favour some degree of government intervention to achieve equality of opportunity.

'Not nearly so pneumatic as Lenina. Oh, not nearly.'

'But old clothes are beastly,' continued the untiring whisper. 'We always throw away old clothes. Ending is better than mending, ending is better than mending, ending is better …'

QUESTION

How do you react to the split narrative of Chapter 3? Does it create a worthwhile effect on the reader or is it merely confusing?

Chapter 3 continues the explanations about the World State which were begun in the first two chapters, but also puts before us particular characters whose stories we shall follow further later. While Mustapha Mond, the Resident Controller for Western Europe, lectures the Hatchery students about the origins and institutions of their society, his speech is interrupted by dramatised reports of his subject matter, by Lenina's conversations with Fanny, and by Bernard's conversations with Henry and the Assistant Predestinator. Some of the interruptions illustrate Mond's ideas, others seem to challenge what he says.

Mond claims that the World State's conditioning system ensures stability of character, yet this is not entirely supported by the evidence. Fanny, it is true, is a strict Alpha, but Lenina has tastes in men which are quite unorthodox. She has a tendency towards monogamy and, when pressed to be more promiscuous, chooses as a partner the unpopular Bernard, just as later she will be drawn to the outsider John. Bernard himself is a more self-conscious dissenter from society, contrasting with the aggressively normal Henry. It is not only his 'ugly' and 'stunted' appearance which cause Bernard's hostility to the system, but his professional familiarity with sleep-teaching, which prevents him from taking seriously such axioms as 'Everyone belongs to everyone else'

In addition to supplying **characterisation**, this chapter gives us a great deal of information. In particular, we learn something of the Nine Years' War and the process by which the World State came into being. It is unlikely that a more straightforward piece of writing would have conveyed this information so well, if only because a step-by-step explanation would have made more glaring the implausibilities of the account. As it is, Huxley makes the least likely events the occasion for his wildest ideas, such as the British Museum Massacre, an incongruous bringing together of the hushed, learned atmosphere of the museum with the colourful violence associated with crime and warfare. The effect is, in a sense, one of **wit**. We appreciate the imaginative daring with which Huxley constructs this world of the future and the elusive tone with which he describes it.

For example, who speaks of the foot landing 'in the middle of the geraniums' (p. 43)? The voice might seem to be Mond's, but as there are no quotation marks it is more likely to be the narrator's. If so, should we infer that the narrator is **sarcastically** amplifying Mond's attitudes to bring out the Controller's wickedness, or offering a viewpoint of his own? Is the tone ghoulishly comic or is it **ironic**? The rapid movement from a chemical formula, through the cold description of mutilation, ending in a flippant **onomatopoeia** ('flop') and a posh-sounding exclamation from an unknown character ('such a splendid show that summer!'), leaves us unsure how to react. As the narrative jumps from one voice to another, the reader is challenged to keep alert and keep thinking. In this story, uncritical acceptance of the narrator's views will not be an option.

As the voices of the citizens of the future and of the sleep-teaching blend together, they lose their individuality and become the collective expression of a cultural disaster which has destroyed the world we know and created a warped and alien successor which we can understand only with an effort. The simultaneous telling of the story from several viewpoints also seems to be a way for Huxley to show off his skills as a writer and establish his credentials as a thoroughly modern artist. The effect might loosely be compared to that of a cubist painting which builds up a picture of an object by fusing together fragmentary images of it, or an early jazz performance in which the lead instruments play different melodies at the same time. It may also recall the multiple narratives of experimental writers of the early 1930s like the American novelists John Dos Passos and William Faulkner. The rapid switching from one speech to another makes unusual demands on the reader, but this in itself is liable to increase our interest in the text. Because we have to make an effort to follow what is happening, we naturally assume that we must take it seriously and reflect thoughtfully upon it.

 CHECK THE BOOK
Examples of similar 'multiple narratives' are *The Sound and the Fury* (1929) and *As I Lay Dying* (1930) by William Faulkner, and *The USA Trilogy* (1930–36) by John Dos Passos.

TEXT 3 – CHAPTER 18 (PP. 227–8)

'Good-morning, Mr Savage,' he said. 'I am the representative of *The Hourly Radio.*'

Startled as though by the bite of a snake, the Savage sprang to his feet, scattering arrows, feathers, glue-pot and brushes in all directions.

'I beg your pardon,' said the reporter, with genuine compunction. 'I had no intention ...' He touched his hat – the aluminium stove-pipe hat in which he carried his wireless receiver and transmitter. 'Excuse my not taking it off,' he said. 'It's a bit heavy. Well, as I was saying, I am the representative of *The Hourly ...*'

'What do you want?' asked the Savage, scowling. The reporter returned his most ingratiating smile.

'Well, of course, our readers would be profoundly interested ...' He put his head on one side, his smile became almost coquettish. 'Just a few words from you, Mr Savage.' And rapidly, with a series of ritual gestures, he uncoiled two wires and connected the portable battery buckled round his waist; plugged them simultaneously into the sides of his aluminium hat; touched a spring on the crown – and antennae sprang up into the air; touched another spring on the peak of the brim – and, like a jack-in-the-box, out jumped a microphone and hung there, quivering, six inches in front of his nose; pulled down a pair of receivers over his ears; pressed a switch on the left side of the hat – and from within came a faint waspy buzzing; turned a knob on the right – and the buzzing was interrupted by a stethoscopic wheeze and crackle, by hiccoughs and sudden squeaks. 'Hullo,' he said to the microphone, 'hullo, hullo ...' A bell suddenly rang inside his hat. 'Is that you, Edzel? Primo Mellon speaking. Yes, I've got hold of him. Mr Savage will now take the microphone and say a few words. Won't you, Mr Savage?' He looked up at the Savage with another of those winning smiles of his. 'Just tell our readers why you came here. What made you leave London (hold on, Edzel!) so very suddenly. And, of course, that whip.' (The Savage started. How did they know about the whip?)

? QUESTION

How does Huxley's use of language contribute to the effectiveness of the novel?

'We're all crazy to know about the whip. And then something about Civilization. You know the sort of stuff. "What I think of the Civilized Girl." Just a few words, a very few ...'

The Savage obeyed with a disconcerting literalness. Five words he uttered and no more – five words, the same as those he had said to Bernard about the Arch-Community-Songster of Canterbury. '*Háni! Sons éso tse-ná!*' And seizing the reporter by the shoulder, he spun him round (the young man revealed himself invitingly well-covered), aimed and, with all the force and accuracy of a champion foot-and-mouth-baller, delivered a most prodigious kick.

Eight minutes later, a new edition of *The Hourly Radio* was on sale in the streets of London. 'HOURLY RADIO REPORTER HAS COCCYX KICKED BY MYSTERY SAVAGE', ran the headlines on the front page. 'SENSATION IN SURREY'.

'Sensation even in London,' thought the reporter when, on his return, he read the words. And a very painful sensation, what was more. He sat down gingerly to his luncheon.

There are many examples of **satire** in *Brave New World*. This depiction of intrusive journalism, from the final chapter of the book, is one of the most conspicuous and memorable of them.

CHECK THE FILM

For those unfamiliar with the silent comedies of the 1920s, entertaining examples include Buster Keaton's *Sherlock Junior* (1924) and *The General* (1926), and Harold Lloyd's *Safety Last* (1923) and *The Freshman* (1925).

The initial comparison of the reporter to a snake suggests that he may be dangerous – even, like the serpent in the Garden of Eden, a tempter who draws people to their own destruction. The snake reference suggests, additionally, a contrast between the ultra-modern world of Surrey (nearby are 'the seven skyscrapers which constituted Guildford', p. 223) and the primitive world of the New Mexican Reservation in Chapter 7, where snakes were such a prominent feature. In the Britain of the future, danger does not come from the natural appetites of wild creatures, we discover, but from a frivolous and artificial demand for fresh 'news', a demand irrelevant to people's actual needs. In our own day of telephoto lenses and bugging devices, this satire has lost none of its force.

Much of the humour of the episode is of a **slapstick** kind, reminiscent of the silent comedy films of the 1920s, from John's initial reaction, through the preposterous mechanical props, to the reporter's violent removal from the scene. With his tall metal hat which converts into an outside broadcast unit, and his ingratiating manner, presuming on a non-existent friendship, Primo Mellon is a delightful **caricature** of an investigative journalist. The long sentence which describes his actions, beginning 'And rapidly', is built around a series of verbs which emphasise his abrupt and ridiculous actions. The incongruous **imagery** of rituals, a jack-in-the-box, wasps, stethoscopes and hiccoughs enhances the absurdity of this performance.

The reference to his 'invitingly well-covered' backside, to which John then proceeds to administer a fierce kick, is just one example of the references to bottoms and whippings which recur throughout the book. Others include the Director's patting of Lenina in Chapter 1, the buttock-drumming of the Solidarity Service in Chapter 5, Helmholtz's poetical praise of 'posteriors' in Chapter 12 and John's assault on Lenina in Chapter 13. Some readers will find it a rather childish subject for humour, others a legitimate way of comically undercutting the pretensions of the World State and ensuring that the book is not narrowly intellectual in its approach to its subject.

The incident between John and Primo Mellon comes after the philosophical discussions with Mond and before the book's horrific ending. Does it detract from the seriousness of these episodes, or does it offer us a moment of **comic relief** between them? It is up to the individual reader to decide. There are many such moments in the book, however – from the Director's waking of the children in Chapter 2 to the **burlesque** fight in Chapter 15 – and an account of it which omitted them and portrayed *Brave New World* as a solemn treatise would be highly misleading.

CONTEXT
Huxley's obsession with bottoms and comic violence is still evident in his 1961 interview where his endorsement of satire concludes: 'I'm all for sticking pins into Episcopal behinds.'

CRITICAL APPROACHES

QUESTION

How effectively
does Huxley depict
character in the
novel?

CHARACTERISATION

Many novels encourage us to engage with the experiences of the
characters and reflect on their behaviour almost as if they were real
people. However, in *Brave New World*, even the most prominent
characters are comparatively simple in conception and predictable
in behaviour. Bernard is always trying crudely to assert himself and
overcome his self-doubt; John is constantly naive and idealistic.
Huxley himself admitted that flat **characterisation** was one of his
chief limitations as a novelist, and that his works of fiction also
contained an unusual amount of essay-like discussion. However,
in the case of *Brave New World* at least, these features are not
necessarily drawbacks. It is arguable that, in portraying a world in
which individuality has been eroded, it is highly appropriate for
characterisation to be quite simple. It is also normal for a work of
dystopian science fiction to emphasise ideas at least as much as
characters, because the interest of such a book lies in its thought-
provoking social speculations, not its insights into everyday life
(see **Literary background**).

According to Donald Watt ('The Manuscript Revisions of *Brave
New World*', 1978, in Meckier, 1996; see **Critical history**), Huxley at
first intended to make Bernard the hero of the book, then introduced
John to take over this role. He eventually decided to give both of
them weaknesses of character which would complicate our attitude
towards their rebellions. Clearly Huxley did not want this to be a
book with a conventional hero, or even villain. Such figures would
create the impression of an entirely straightforward contrast between
good and evil, whereas Huxley wished to explore difficult issues and
encourage the reader to think them through. The characters are as
much vehicles for this process as ends in themselves.

BERNARD MARX

Bernard Marx is the main character in the first part of the book.
He works in the Psychology Bureau, where he is an expert in

76 Brave New World

sleep-teaching. Compared to his fellow Alpha Pluses, he is stunted and even ugly, allegedly because his development was affected at the embryo stage by a misdirected dose of the alcohol used to reduce the quality of lower caste embryos. His physical difference has given Bernard an inferiority complex. As he puts it in Chapter 4, section 2, 'I am I, and wish I wasn't' (p. 57). He resents other Alphas whom he suspects of feeling superior to him, and he also fears being mocked by members of the lower classes. This alienation from society causes him to value solitude and independence. Because of his feelings of exclusion and his familiarity with the indoctrination process, Bernard also has a critical attitude towards people who are well adjusted and, with it, a willingness to express unorthodox views. He is curious about other ways of life and eager to visit the Savage Reservation, but ultimately he is not opposed to the World State and its regulation of the individual, only resentful at his own failure to fit comfortably into the system.

In some respects this hostility is unconvincing. A dose of alcohol at the embryo stage might have affected his intelligence or abilities, but how could it make him embarrassed by the mating customs of his own society, as he is in Chapter 3 and at the beginning of Chapter 4? His feelings here seem to be those of a twentieth-century person projected crudely into the future. We disregard this flaw in the logic of the book, however, because we are amused by Bernard's mischievous, bungling behaviour and his comical lapses into the role of victim.

Bernard seems to desire a loving relationship with Lenina, and he is attracted to the other dissidents, Helmholtz and John. However, he is too selfish to be a true friend to anyone. We learn in Chapter 12 that he is a person for whom any friend is actually a 'victim-friend' (p. 162), a convenient target for resentments which he cannot otherwise express. His insecurity makes him inconsistent, boastful, self-pitying and disloyal. When he temporarily gets the chance to mix with social superiors and sleep with lots of women, he soon forgets his criticisms of society, which are mainly based on negative feelings, not reasoned argument. At times Bernard acts from conviction, but at others he is weak and easily overcome, so that we have to regard him as his own worst enemy.

CHECK THE FILM

In Michael R. Joyce's 1998 film adaptation of *Brave New World*, Bernard and John are made much more like conventional heroes, without personal defects that undermine their positive qualities.

Because we sympathise with Bernard's views without endorsing him as our representative, Huxley is able to get the best of both worlds. We share Bernard's disgust at the shallow, promiscuous behaviour of the others, yet we laugh at his jealous, hypocritical reactions. By the time he is exiled, near the end of the book, our interest in his fate has diminished and we have become much more concerned about what will happen to John.

JOHN, THE SAVAGE

Like Bernard, John is an outsider in a world of conformists. He has grown up with a European appearance in a New Mexican village, where his mother's sexual promiscuity has made him doubly an outcast. The religion of the tribe is a composite of pagan and Christian mythology, and John's immersion in the writings of Shakespeare has added a further cultural dimension to his outlook which makes it absolutely unique, leaving him equally ill at ease with life in the Reservation and in the World State.

As was the case with Bernard, defects in John's personality tend to undermine our faith in his views. In particular, in **farcical** conformity to the theories of Freudian psychology, his relationship with his mother has impaired his sexual development. Having rejected her promiscuity and turned to an ideal of chastity deduced from passages in Shakespeare, he is unable to respond to the open sexuality of Lenina, the one human being for whom he feels passion, except with alarm, rejection and finally violence. Indeed, from early childhood his sexual feelings seem to have been perverted into violence against himself, seen in his practice of beating himself with a whip, his self-induced vomiting and his final self-destruction.

CHECK THE BOOK

John Carey's *The Intellectuals and the Masses: Pride and Prejudice Among the Literary Intelligentsia, 1800–1939* (1992) groups Huxley with intellectuals of the period who looked down on ordinary people.

It must be said that, like Bernard, John is not an entirely convincing character. Huxley concedes in his Foreword to the book that John's style of reasoning is at odds with his primitive upbringing. John Carey has complained that the Savage displays 'the inhibitions and cultural preferences of a late nineteenth-century public schoolboy' (Carey, 1992; see **Critical history**). Huxley's failure to establish the integrity of his central character may be judged a significant flaw in the book, especially in Chapter 17 where, in the debate with Mond, he has great difficulty in maintaining John's normal style of speech. However, we must remember that we are not reading a realistic novel. *Brave New World* has to maintain a balance between storytelling and discussion, and arguably the characters are sufficiently credible to serve their purpose in this context. Indeed, if we had more empathy with John, we should be too upset by his suffering to maintain the detached attitude required by Huxley's **satire**, and we would therefore lose our sense of the book's overall argument.

John's presence helps call into question many aspects of life in the World State and the points he voices raise questions about its values and philosophy. However, we cannot assume that John is a reliable mouthpiece for Huxley's own views and that these can be accepted uncritically as the book's 'message'. While Huxley may have expected us to share John's distaste for the World State and sympathise with his rebellion against it, he cannot have intended us to share his eccentric religious affiliations to Pookong and the eagle, or to admire the way he whips himself. John is intentionally a very flawed hero.

QUESTION

How far does Huxley succeed in making the relationships between his main characters credible?

LENINA CROWNE

Lenina is 'uncommonly pretty' (Chapter 1, p. 13) and she is desired by many men, including Bernard and John. In a conventional novel, this would lead to conflict between them, but here it serves as a way to link their two stories and unify the book.

In some ways Lenina is a model citizen of the future. She does not question society consciously. When we first see her she is giving the Director a 'rather deferential smile' (Chapter 1, p. 13) and her favourite words of criticism are 'odd' and 'queer'. Her past relationships have been so shallow that in Chapter 6 she cannot remember who it was who took her for a weekend to New York. However, despite herself, Lenina frequently deviates from the requirements of the World State, feeling curiosity about the Savage Reservation, showing monogamous feelings towards Henry Foster, taking pity on Bernard for his inadequacies, being rather repelled by the Arch-Community-Songster of Canterbury and being fascinated by the unorthodox attitudes of John, for whom in Chapter 12 she even comes to feel old-fashioned sensations of love. She receives limited development as a personality in her own right, however, and functions largely as a **foil** for the chief male characters.

MUSTAPHA MOND

Mustapha Mond is the Resident Controller for Western Europe. His appearance is described early in Chapter 3. He contributes two lengthy expositions to the book in Chapters 3 and 16–17, explaining the theory and practice of the World State. As a scientist, he was once a potential rebel against the state, but he chose power and responsibility above the chance to advance human knowledge. In **plot** terms, he is the villain of the book, but Huxley carefully gives him persuasive arguments and a calm, rational personality, both of which might be considered rather attractive when compared to the excitable and impulsive behaviour of Bernard and John. Like Lenina, Mond is developed to only a limited extent and functions largely as a foil to those whom he has arrested, his career development contrasting with Helmholtz's, his religious views with John's.

CHECK THE FILM

In Michael R. Joyce's 1998 film adaptation of *Brave New World*, because Bernard and John are comparatively heroic in character, Helmholtz is redundant and does not appear.

HELMHOLTZ WATSON

Helmholtz Watson is the character who is presented most positively. The main account of him comes at the end of Chapter 4. He is strong, handsome, intelligent and talented. Whereas Bernard and John become rebels due to their inability to fit into the World State, Helmholtz is successful in his career and is also an 'indefatigable lover' (Chapter 4, section 2, p. 60). His rebellion, which is calmer and more thoughtful than theirs, is prompted by his sense that human existence has more to offer than the state allows. He is a good friend to Bernard and John, forgiving the former when he behaves badly and going to the latter's aid in the brawl at the Hospital. His departure to the Falklands to write poetry represents a limited creative dissent which is perhaps the only sign of hope in the novel. Huxley is careful not to allow Helmholtz to appear frequently or initiate much action, presumably because he does not want the book to have a hero with whom we might unthinkingly identify.

THE DIRECTOR

The tour of the Hatchery with which the book opens establishes its Director, Thomas, as a domineering type who likes the sound of his own voice. He smiles at the students with 'a slightly menacing geniality' (Chapter 1, p. 2), but puts on a different expression to ingratiate himself with Mond, 'smiling with all his teeth, effusive' (Chapter 3, p. 29). Even his initials endorsing a letter by the Controller are 'two small pale letters abject at the feet of Mustapha Mond' (Chapter 6, section 2, p. 85). A total conformist, unable to cope with any deviation from normal behaviour, he is disturbed by Mond's wide-ranging talk to the students in Chapter 3. **Ironically** he is eventually humiliated because of his own past unorthodoxy. It seems that in a world where everyone is supposed to have been programmed, even those in charge cannot help betraying their conditioning. His dreams are haunted by feelings of guilt about leaving Linda to die at the Reservation and, against his own judgement, he experiences an 'inward compulsion' (Chapter 6, section 2, p. 86) to reveal this to Bernard.

CHECK THE FILM
In Michael R. Joyce's 1998 film adaptation of *Brave New World*, the Director is made into a conventional villain. He kills Linda to conceal their relationship and unsuccessfully reprograms a production line worker to kill Bernard. Why do you think these major changes were made?

HENRY FOSTER

Henry is a minor character who demonstrates to us the behaviour of a typical citizen of the World State. In Chapter 1 he enthusiastically supplies information about the workings of the Hatchery. In Chapter 3 he endorses promiscuity and teases Bernard for his deviancy. In Chapter 4 he is contrasted with Bernard in his confidence with women and the lower classes, and is also shown to be an impatient advocate of efficiency, criticising lack of punctuality wherever he sees it. Surprisingly, in Chapter 5, section 1, he reflects sadly on death and points out to Lenina how her opinions have been formed by sleep-teaching, an idea normally expressed by Bernard. Could it be that these lines were originally written for Bernard, then reassigned to Henry? In the final pages of the book Henry demonstrates the shallowness of his relationship with Lenina by abandoning her and hiding behind his helicopter when she is attacked.

LINDA

Introduced in Chapter 7 as a 'very stout blonde squaw' (p. 106), John's mother Linda is ugly, unintelligent and forever out of place. She was originally a Beta who worked in the Fertilizing Room, then she was taken to the Reservation by the Alpha who would later become the Director of Hatcheries and Conditioning. He left her there, believing her to have died in an accident. Her promiscuous modern attitude towards sex causes her to be persecuted by the Savages on the Reservation and, when she returns to the World State, both her physical deterioration and her motherhood make her an object of horror. She turns to *soma* and soon dies in a hallucinatory state. No character in the book shows her any sympathy. Her lover Popé is a possible exception, but her inability to distinguish him in her memory from Waihusiwa (Chapter 7, p. 110) suggests that their relationship was no deeper than the World State norm. John's attempts to show affection for her only express what he believes a son ought to feel, not the thwarted love and resentment which are his real feelings. When these do come out, he shakes her in anger and, by so doing, apparently precipitates her death. The contempt with which everyone in the book regards her may, paradoxically, make the reader sympathise with Linda as someone who has only tried to live as she was taught to do and who does not merit the misfortunes which she suffers.

QUESTION

If someone you know was thinking of reading *Brave New World*, what aspects of the book would you use to recommend it and which aspects might you caution them about?

THEMES

DEHUMANISATION

The central theme of *Brave New World* is dehumanisation. The book suggests that a number of trends in the modern world are eroding the idea of human beings as unique individuals, each with his or her own 'soul' (however defined), and it depicts what might conceivably happen if these trends were to prevail.

From where does the threat to individuality come? Partly it is a result of living in a large, complex society in which for much of the time we have to relate to each other on a mass scale through impersonal institutions. Advertisers, employers, psychologists, politicians and others find it convenient to group people into categories by factors such as personality types, levels of education, jobs and interests. Their criteria turn us from complex individuals into **stereotypical** 'C2s', 'aspirers', 'extroverts' and so on. Once we have been so identified, we can be targeted by advertisements and products which reinforce this limited sense of who we are and encourage us to continue in the same restricted path, with the theoretical risk that our lives could come to be completely predictable and 'packaged'. One of the worst horrors of *Brave New World* is that science has given the Controllers the means to reach into people's personalities and adjust them so that they conform to the categories assigned them. They are now 'Alpha Pluses', 'Epsilon-Minus Semi-Morons' and so on, not simply because they can be grouped like this for particular purposes, but because they have been designed from conception to fit these social groups. The citizens of the World State have no ideas not put into their heads by the Controllers. The mass media, sport, *soma* and other distractions ensure that they have no time for experiences or reflections which might lead them outside the 'package' in which they have been placed.

www. CHECK THE NET
There is a defence of 'paradise engineering' against Huxley's criticisms at **http://www. huxley.net**

Dehumanisation threatens us at a deeper level than social stereotyping, however. The modern age is the age of science, and the concepts of science are general and impersonal. As we have developed scientific understanding of the world around us, so we have had to discard the primitive belief that it is animated by spirits. We no longer see the sun as a god or something miraculous, but as a ball of gases which obeys physical laws. Since Darwin's work on evolution, scientific explanations have more and more been applied to human behaviour, which is also conceived of as part of nature. Aldous Huxley's grandfather, the distinguished scientist T. H. Huxley, even suggested in his book *Method and Results* (1893) that science might one day reveal human beings to be conscious machines, their thoughts no more in control of their actions than the smoke from a factory chimney is in control of the factory's operations. *Brave New World* shows us a society where people have been so influenced by such ideas that they have begun to treat each other like machines and behave accordingly. 'The fifty-six four-spindle chucking and turning machines were being manipulated by fifty-six aquiline and ginger Gammas' (Chapter 11, p. 144).

TRUE AND FALSE SCIENCE

Huxley was not opposed to scientific knowledge or methods, only to the assumption that science offers a standpoint from which everything can easily be understood and all problems solved. In his book *Literature and Science* (1963) Huxley describes science, from the novelist's point of view, as 'a treasure of newly discovered facts and tentative hypotheses'. *Brave New World* is, among other things, an attack on people who offer the public ambitious, all-encompassing systems of ideas which are supposed to be based on science, but which, on inspection, turn out to lack its tentative, hypothetical regard for truth, relying instead on simplistic, mechanistic views of human nature. The most prominent of Huxley's targets here are Henry Ford, Sigmund Freud and J. B. Watson.

Watson, a behaviourist psychologist, tried to reduce all human activity to a pattern of physical 'stimulus' and 'response'. He attached so little importance to inner activities like imagination and reason, and so much to the influence of the environment, that he boasted in his book *Behaviorism* (1925):

> Give me a dozen healthy infants, well-formed, and my own specified world to bring them up in and I'll guarantee to take any one at random and train him to become any type of specialist I might select … regardless of his talents, penchants, tendencies, abilities, vocations, and race of his ancestors.

Even the Director of Hatcheries does not go this far in downplaying people's innate characteristics. The Director has at least the sense to choose appropriate genetic material before subjecting the infants to behaviourist conditioning.

CONTEXT

In an interview Huxley remarked: 'The trouble with Freudian psychology is that it is based exclusively on a study of the sick. Freud never met a healthy human being – only patients and other psychoanalysts.'

Freud's approach to psychology might seem to be the opposite of Watson's, placing far more emphasis on inner experience, but Huxley points out in Chapter 8 of his novel *Island* that both psychoanalysis and behaviourism are highly general theories which ignore 'the built-in, congenital differences between individuals' and regard people as mere victims of their experiences. Like Watson, Freud reduces human activity to a comparatively simple proposition, this time that it is dominated by so-called 'sexual' energy which bad experiences can divert into damaging channels, rather like water running astray in a piece of hydraulic machinery. It is not possible to see any evidence of this process, nor is it permissible for people to solve their problems themselves. Instead, they have passively to submit themselves to lengthy repair by an approved expert. In *Brave New World*, the World State has overcome the need for even this much respect for the individual by abolishing the family, which Freud saw as the prime source of inner conflict, and encouraging everyone to have sex with everyone else, thus removing sexual frustration – the kind of policies which were in fact advocated by some radical Freudians in the 1960s. Only John the Savage still has Freudian neurosis, and his unusual circumstances and eccentric actions serve as another way for Huxley to mock Freud's ideas as one-sided and exaggerated.

The last of the three influential thinkers whom the book **satirises** is Henry Ford, the American car manufacturer who pioneered mass production. Ford raised the pay of his workers and reduced the cost of cars so that ordinary people could afford them, but there was a downside to his achievement in that he treated his workers almost as though they were themselves machines. His production lines required workers to carry out the same limited tasks over and over again. Worse, Ford expected his workers to behave as he dictated not only in his factory, but in their homes and leisure time, and sent out company spies to make sure that they did so.

These three systems of ideas, important and influential in different ways but all much more limited in application than their founders claimed, are attractive to the World State Controllers because they offer a coherent framework for stability, whereas genuine scientific research is a dynamic force which is unpredictable and so constantly challenges existing social arrangements and ideas. Mustapha Mond states clearly in Chapter 16 that 'high art' and scientific research alike are explorations of reality which conflict with social stability, therefore they have to be eradicated.

DEATH

The World State lives in denial of the experiences which are central to art: namely, love, conflict, suffering and death – yet death in particular is never far off, especially in the **imagery** of the book, from the 'corpse-coloured rubber' of the workers' gloves in Chapter 1 (p. 1) to the hanging corpse which ends Chapter 18. This is partly **symbolic**. It suggests that the dehumanised life of A.F. 632 is itself a kind of living death because the people of the future are

> **CONTEXT**
>
> Today the word 'Fordism' is sometimes used to describe the stage-by-stage manufacture of standardised products on a production line in large factories, manned by full-time male workers whose wages are set through collective bargaining. It is sometimes claimed that we now live in a period of 'post-Fordism', characterised by a more varied range of products aimed at 'niche markets', produced by a more diverse workforce dominated by part-time female workers, for sophisticated consumers who cannot easily be categorised into simple social classes. If it is true that these social changes have occurred, it might make some of Huxley's satire less relevant today than it was in the 'Fordist' 1930s.

cut off from the natural experiences needed for fulfilment. More literally, it reminds us that death is inevitable and, to be fully human, we have to come to terms with it in some meaningful way. The irrational rites of the Reservation may not much impress us as a religious solution, but even they may be more satisfactory than what happens at the Park Lane Hospital for the Dying, which 'hushes up' death in a way not perhaps so different from present-day customs.

LACK OF A POSITIVE MESSAGE

John draws attention to the absence of a religious awareness which would enable the citizens of the World State to face up to death more fully, but his own attempts to supply a better perspective are unimpressive. This lack of a positive 'message' in the book may be considered a problem, as it is by Huxley in his Foreword. However, *Brave New World* may be read as an **ironic** narrative, like Swift's *Gulliver's Travels* (1726) or Wells's *The Island of Doctor Moreau* (1896), one where every positive idea is deliberately undermined somewhere else in the story. Such a book does not pretend to offer firm conclusions, but treats the issues raised as genuinely difficult ones which readers have to think about for themselves.

CHECK THE BOOK

Jonathan Swift's *Gulliver's Travels* and H. G. Wells's *The Island of Doctor Moreau* are disturbing satirical fantasies which can be compared to *Brave New World*.

One point which may occur to us when we do think about the book's implications is that *Brave New World* is remarkably uninformative about the World State's political arrangements. How do the Controllers retain their commanding power? How do they delegate decision-making downwards? Who initiates and implements the policies mentioned in the book, such as the abolition of the love of nature among the lower classes (Chapter 2) or the Cyprus experiment (Chapter 16)? It could be argued that the omission of these political details is unrealistic. On the other hand, Huxley may actually be making a political point, that the long-term tendency to treat people like machines exists regardless of the politics which prevail – capitalist or Communist, democratic or totalitarian.

The themes of *Brave New World* are so prominent and important that it is easy to discuss the book as though it were an essay, not a work of fiction. Like all **utopias** and **dystopias**, and much **science** fiction, it is a book which resists being confined within the category of 'literature' and demands we reflect fairly directly upon its truth to life. Nonetheless, the success of the book depends upon the skill with which it has been constructed and anyone who is studying it as part of a literature course will need to be able to discuss this intelligently. How does Huxley try to make his future world credible and his ideas dramatically effective? Students need to be able to discuss the experience of reading the book, not just list key features of the World State.

LANGUAGE AND STYLE

**CHECK
THE BOOK**

Dennis Freeborn's *Style: Text Analysis and Linguistic Criticism* (1996) is a useful general read on language and style.

As in any **science fiction** portrayal of a world different from our own, there is much to be explained, and as in any **novel of ideas** (see **Literary background**), there is much to be discussed. Some of the book's characters, therefore – in particular, the Director, Mond and Foster – make lengthy speeches which are more like lectures than ordinary talk, using specialist jargon, signposting of key points and rhetorical questions. Some readers will feel that these passages awkwardly hold up the story but, as well as supplying information which we need to know, they manifest the power structure of the World State, where those in charge speak authoritatively and those below listen and are occasionally allowed to put questions.

The narration and description of the book are brisk, with much use of **ellipsis, parenthesis** and informal sentence structures (many sentences begin with 'And' and 'But', and even 'Which' and 'Because'). These features take us rapidly from one idea to the next, and from one person's perceptions to the next, building up an overview and conveying the fantastic events too quickly and in a tone too matter-of-fact for us to question them.

Parody is another major stylistic feature, with Huxley imitating the language of, for instance, upper-class slang, pop songs, religion, bureaucracy and science. In addition to being an entertaining aspect of the book, this feature demonstrates that, just as the World State equips its citizens with parodies of art and religion, so it equips them with a parody of meaningful discourse. When faced with any

CONTEXT

The poet William
Blake (1757–1827)
observed that 'the
sayings used in a
nation mark its
character'. This is
the belief which
lies behind
Huxley's inclusion
of sayings from
the World State.

situation, its people are incapable of an original response and simply
fall back on clichés from advertising slogans, nursery rhymes and
proverbs, many of them corruptions of ancient ones which have
been rewritten by Helmholtz and his fellow 'emotional engineers':
'Safe as helicopters', 'Ending is better than mending', 'Everyone
belongs to everyone else'.

Like Newspeak, the 'official language' of George Orwell's *Nineteen
Eighty-Four*, the proverbial sayings of the World State are a way
to reinforce orthodox ideas and make it hard to conceive of
alternatives ones. We learn in Chapter 3 that the words 'mother',
'father', 'parent', 'family', 'home', 'born', 'monogamy', 'romance',
'Christianity' and 'parliament' have all become obsolete and some
of them have now become taboo words with the power to shock.
Overall, the ideal seems to be for humans to achieve the predictable,
standardised discourse of a machine, like the synthetic voices we
hear in the Solidarity Service of Chapter 5 and the music box's
'Anti-Riot Speech Number Two (Medium Strength)' in Chapter 15
(p. 196). Mond's oratory, we are assured, is 'almost up to synthetic
standards' (Chapter 16, p. 202).

Helmholtz complains that such plain and predictable language
is incapable of poetry. When John reads him Shakespeare, he
recognises that the 'old fellow' (Chapter 12, p. 166) achieves the
power of language which he cannot ('Words can be like X-rays …
piercing', Chapter 4, section 2, p. 62), because Shakespeare lived in
a comparatively primitive society where individuals experienced
thoroughgoing passions. For John, on the other hand, who has
grown up in an extremely primitive society and resorts to Zuñi
obscenities to express his disgust, Shakespeare's language is that of
an advanced, reflective civilisation. It seems that a balance has to be
struck between the primitive and the sophisticated in order for
culture to achieve greatness.

If Huxley is suggesting that the culture of his own time has already
become too cut off from natural experiences to retain its poetic
capacity, he nonetheless draws upon the most prominent poet in
English of the era, T. S. Eliot, for some of his language. The
euphemism 'pneumatic' is taken from Eliot's 'Whispers of

Immortality' (1918) and the use of Sir Alfred Mond as a figure of satire from 'A Cooking Egg' (1919). In many of his poems, particularly *The Waste Land* (1922), Eliot mingles quotations from classic texts like Shakespeare with sordid or commonplace language from the present, creating the impression that modern civilisation is inferior when judged against the achievements of the past. Huxley seems to use Shakespeare in the same way in *Brave New World*. However, the method of allusion requires active interpretation by the reader. Some critics have assumed that Shakespeare must be good and modernity bad, but the text invites a more discriminating reading. While Shakespeare certainly offers a standard of sensitivity and eloquence against which the culture of the Reservation, the World State and the reader's own world can be judged, John's use of Shakespearean quotation is anything but creative. In fact, it oddly parallels the World State habit of falling back on slogans in place of thought. John's recourse to Shakespeare is sometimes a legitimate way to articulate feelings which he would otherwise be unable to express, but there are contrasting times when John seems to be using the quotations as a way of claiming unearned superiority, parroting the words without understanding their full meaning. He is factually wrong in confusing Ariel and the Puck in Chapter 11, but he is even more wrong in stereotyping Lenina as possessing 'vestal modesty' (Chapter 9, p. 130). He later calls her an 'Impudent strumpet!' (Chapter 13, p. 176), which is what the murderously jealous Othello calls the innocent Desdemona. If he understood his Shakespeare more thoroughly, John might pause and realise that the words contain a warning about his own tendency to swing unchecked from love to hatred.

Huxley's own opinions are expressed less through the Shakespeare quotations than in the imagery used throughout the book to support the theme of dehumanisation. T. H. Huxley once suggested that utopias were incompatible with human nature and more suited to insects (see **Intertextuality**). It is fitting therefore that his grandson's futuristic civilisation is characterised by images of pestilence. In Chapter 4 the Charing-T Tower is like a fungus and, seen from a helicopter, people look like maggots, locusts, aphids and ants, an insect comparison repeated many times later in the book. It is also possible for these images to be read oppositionally, however,

CHECK THE BOOK

John Carey in *The Intellectuals and the Masses: Pride and Prejudice Among the Literary Intelligentsia, 1800–1939* (1992) brackets together Huxley and T. S. Eliot as upper-class intellectuals hostile to the 'masses', both, for example, opposed to academic education being open to everyone.

as a symptom of Huxley's contempt for ordinary people (see **Social background**). As noted above in **Themes**, from first page to last, the book presents us with images of death, suggesting that the World State's citizens are more like zombies or robots than people able to live life fully. In Chapter 2 the Hatchery babies are 'pale as death' (p. 16) and European languages other than English are 'dead' (p. 20). In Chapter 3 we learn of the horrors of the Nine Years' War and also see Lenina spray talcum powder over herself from a nozzle 'as though she meant to commit suicide' (p. 32). The deathly imagery is not confined to the World State, but is also applied to the Reservation where a dog lies dead on a rubbish heap (Chapter 7) and John recalls being driven out into a 'skeleton world' in 'dead light' (Chapter 8, p. 124).

NARRATIVE TECHNIQUE AND STRUCTURE

The book's structure is a simple and logical one. The first three chapters explain the nature of the World State and offer us an initial glimpse of the characters. The speed and ingenuity of the ideas which are advanced here keep the reader interested, as does the increasing emphasis on the characters in Chapter 3. With the general way of life of the World State established, full attention is given to the characters in Chapters 4 to 6. The trip to the Reservation introduces an alternative society in Chapters 7 to 9. In Chapters 10 to 15 John moves from the Reservation to the World State and reacts to it. Chapters 16 and 17 report the debate between John and Mond. Chapter 18 concludes with John's withdrawal from society and his failure to achieve a sane existence on his own. Within this structure, Huxley develops a number of dramatic contrasts such as the two air journeys in Chapter 4, which display the different mentalities of Henry and Bernard, and the fertility ceremony in Chapter 7, which contrasts with the Solidarity Service in Chapter 5 and with the fertilisation arrangements in Chapter 1, as well as prefiguring the beating and self-destruction of Chapter 18.

A constantly shifting point of view, often achieved through **free indirect discourse**, makes for a fast-moving, fluid narrative, which repeatedly dissolves the author's opinions into those of the

CHECK THE BOOK
There is a good introduction to narrative techniques in Section 5 of *Ways of Reading: Advanced Readings Skills for Students of English Literature* by Martin Montgomery, Alan Durant, Nigel Fabb, Tom Furniss and Sarah Mills (1992).

characters. The second section of Chapter 4, for example, starts by describing and analysing Bernard from the outside, but the second paragraph takes us directly into his mind and lets us follow his thoughts, while the third paragraph moves between these two perspectives. When John recalls his childhood with Linda in Chapter 8 we start from Bernard's point of view, contemplating John's account externally as someone unfamiliar with his world, but we soon find ourselves immersed in John's experiences and later, when we churn through a sentence in which 'and' is used twenty-three times, in the rambling thoughts of Linda. The long-term effect of these shifting viewpoints is to leave us with only a general sense of where the author stands. We have to formulate our own final perspective, not rely on Huxley to tell us what to think.

Huxley wrote that 'the comic and the tragic are the same thing seen from different angles. I try to get a stereoscopic vision, to show my characters from two angles simultaneously' (quoted in Watt, 1975; see **Critical history**). One of the most distinctive features of the book is this 'stereoscopic effect', which Huxley believed compensated for his comparatively simple approach to **characterisation**. The neo-Pavlovian torture of the babies in Chapter 2, for example, is undeniably a terrible event, yet it is also presented as a lightly comical scene. Linda is a pitiful victim of everyone she meets and the triggering of her death by her son as he tries to express his love for her should be a moment of excruciating tragedy, but in fact Linda is always seen as laughable and her death is in some respects a piece of **slapstick** humour. Lenina and John are two people who have been so warped by their upbringing in different cultures that they cannot express their love for each other, and their relationship ends in shocking violence, yet this is used as a source of knockabout comedy. Readers will differ in their response to these scenes, but even those who find them distasteful rather than interestingly complex will have to agree that they do convey forcibly a sense of cultural relativism. The outlooks of the Reservation, the World State and our own period are not easy to reconcile, and the book reinforces this point by presenting us with material about which it is not easy to have a straightforward response.

CHECK THE BOOK

For a wide-ranging discussion of sources and contexts, see Peter Firchow's *The End of Utopia: A Study of Aldous Huxley's Brave New World* (1984).

**CHECK
THE BOOK**

H. G. Wells's *Men
Like Gods* was the
original target of
Huxley's satire in
Brave New World.

SATIRE

Brave New World began, Huxley told interviewers, as 'a **parody**
of H. G. Wells's *Men Like Gods* (1923), but gradually it got out
of hand' (Plimpton, 1963; see **Critical history**). The resemblance
between the two books remains clear. *Men Like Gods* depicts a
world in which a **utopian** social system has been created after five
centuries of war. It maintains itself through eugenic breeding and
careful education. Politics, business competition and private wealth
have all been 'laid aside'. The action of the book concerns a number
of intruders, based upon well-known public figures of the 1920s,
who disagree with the principles of this utopia and come into
violent conflict with it.

One target of Huxley's **satire** is the ideals of 'progressive' thinkers
like Wells who proposed that scientific innovation and a shift in
social organisation from the individual to the collective would bring
about a much better world for humanity. *Brave New World*
suggests that this is a naive view and that such a change might
instead bring about uniformity, passivity and spiritual
impoverishment. However, Huxley mocks as perhaps more
inadequate still the Romantic alternative of rejecting science and
embracing 'nature', a view most powerfully exemplified in his own
day by his friend D. H. Lawrence. For Huxley the World State
(a term which Wells often used for his utopias) and the New
Mexican Indians (whose ways of life Lawrence discussed in his
1927 book *Mornings in Mexico*) offer two interesting, but ultimately
false, goals. *Brave New World* is designed to mock and discredit
both of these proposed solutions for the ills of civilisation.

At the same time, Huxley's satire also highlights those ills. **Social
background** discusses in more detail how the mass culture of
modern capitalist society is **caricatured** in several features of the
World State, a world in which recreation, gossip-based journalism,
religion and careerism occupy people so much that they never have
time to reflect on who is controlling their behaviour and why. In
some respects Huxley's critical view is at least as relevant now as it
was when the book was published in 1932, since today journalism is

arguably more intrusive, the cinema more pornographic and drug abuse more widespread.

In other respects, however, the book has dated. Some of the scientific speculation which was futuristic in 1932 now seems quaint. A modern reader will be surprised to find that the embryos on the production line are serviced by people, not by computerised machines which would be able to measure out dosages much more accurately. Equally surprisingly, Bernard has to undertake a long helicopter journey to communicate with Mond because he has no mobile phone, and sleep-teaching is not recorded electronically, but on paper sound-track rolls.

Much more damagingly, although the shifting points of view of the narrative make it difficult to tell which attitudes are those of the narrator and which those of the characters, a modern reader is likely to be suspicious that Huxley endorses several attitudes which today we would condemn. The references to the 'negro ovary' (Chapter 1, p. 6), the 'enormous negro dove' (5, p. 76) and the 'gigantic Negro' (Chapter 11, p. 151) all constitute racial **stereotyping**. The descriptions of the Epsilon-Minus liftman (Chapter 4) and of the Deltas at the Hospital ('less than human monsters', Chapter 15, p. 194) make contemptuous fun of people who are not only disabled but who have been disabled deliberately, an attitude we might well not regard as funny. The rather gloating descriptions of women's bodies, such as 'the firm and sunburnt flesh of eighty superb female specimens' (Chapter 3, p. 31), are not so much sexist as off-puttingly juvenile in tone. We may find, also, that we do not share Huxley's apparent shock at the recycling of human remains, the use of contraception outside marriage or the staging of women's wrestling. One feminist has actually endorsed the negative description of family life in Chapter 3 and other readers may approve of the drug-taking and promiscuity practised by the citizens of the future. It is possible to argue that such reactions only prove that Huxley was right in his forecasts, but they also suggest that at least some of the book's satire is bound to lose its impact as times and opinions change.

Perhaps a greater weakness which can be alleged against the satire is that it does not always integrate well with the narrative. Does the

> **CONTEXT**
>
> In an interview Huxley stated: 'I'm all for satire. We need it. People everywhere take things much too seriously, I think.'

satire on journalism in the last chapter supply **comic relief** after the earnest debate between John and Mond and, by so doing, increase the impact of the final horror; or does it have such a light, flippant tone that it actually detracts from the serious events either side of it?

INTERTEXTUALITY

Brave New World frequently draws upon Huxley's wide reading (details of which are discussed in Firchow, 1984; see **Critical history**) and many later writers have in turn been influenced by him. One widespread critical approach to *Brave New World*, therefore, is to compare it to other books, seeing it as part of an ongoing literary debate about human nature and social ideals.

Several critics have suggested that the discussions between John and Mond in Chapters 16 and 17 are indebted to 'The Grand Inquisitor', a chapter from Fyodor Dostoevsky's novel *The Brothers Karamazov* (1880). There is certainly a resemblance, though the two pieces of writing make significantly different points. Dostoevsky's character, Ivan, tells the story of how Jesus returns to this world at the time of the Spanish Inquisition, only to be imprisoned and finally burned to death. The Inquisitor tells Him that most people cannot cope with the freedom He wants to give them and praises the Roman Catholic Church as a conspiracy to replace genuine religion with a world state which will satisfy people's longing for a clear moral framework, at the price of insulating them from a direct relationship with God. Huxley envisages a world still more sinister than this, one where people can no longer even feel the need for spiritual freedom because they have been turned into a new type of creature by biological science.

 CHECK THE BOOK

H. G. Wells's *The Time Machine* is a classic work of science fiction with a strong dystopian element.

The **utopian/dystopian** tradition is a more obvious place to look for comparisons, however, and probably a more profitable one. At the beginning of the twentieth century H. G. Wells's synthesis of utopia, dystopia, the **novel of ideas** and **science fiction** gave people a new way of exploring social trends and ideas of human nature.

Many writers were influenced by Wells's early dystopian science fiction, but were less comfortable with his later utopian emphasis, which they felt was too crudely optimistic and based on a narrow conception of human life. Huxley certainly felt that Wells was inclined to confuse the progress of science, which was indisputable, with the progress of civilisation, which was quite a different issue. In some of his essays Huxley argues that improvements in machinery actually tend to remove people's initiative and limit their range of choices, making them over passive. In his novel *Point Counter Point* (1928), Huxley has one character, Rampion, ridicule Wells's view of evolution for its limited perspective, claiming that it starts with the apes and leads to Wells and Sir Alfred Mond as the ideal human beings.

From Wells's utopian fiction – not only *Men Like Gods* but also *A Modern Utopia* (1905) – Huxley took the idea of a World State set up after the existing order has been wrecked by war and economic collapse, a state which has achieved stability and peace by making radical use of technology and by careful education or indoctrination of its citizens. Other features, however, reach back to Wells's dystopias. The breeding of different social classes recalls the evolution of humanity into different species in *The Time Machine* (1895); their colour-coded clothing derives from *When the Sleeper Wakes* (1899). Perhaps the most interesting link, however, is with *The First Men in the Moon* (1901). When Wells's two space travellers land on the Moon, they discover a lunar civilisation which physically modifies its offspring in order to fit them to society's needs, producing big-headed administrators, musclebound policemen and 'hands' who are merely hands. Curiously, Wells may have been inspired here by Huxley's grandfather. In *Evolution and Ethics* (1894) T. H. Huxley attacked utopianism by arguing that people are individual creatures who co-operate socially because they have shared needs and sympathies. A society where everybody is regulated for the common good could never work in practice because it would undermine the family and destroy social bonding. It could only succeed in a society where each member is biologically predestined to fulfil a particular function, as is the case in a beehive. It was presumably in response to this that Wells made his Moon people insect-like. *Brave New World* radically redevelops this idea by suggesting that scientific progress

 CHECK THE BOOK

H. G. Wells's *The First Men in the Moon* depicts a lunar society which is a forerunner of *Brave New World*.

could one day change human nature so that people become more like insects and grow up biologically specialised, thus making extreme utopianism possible after all.

Because *Brave New World* is part of an ongoing literary debate, students are often asked to compare the book with others, especially George Orwell's *Nineteen Eighty-Four* (1949) and Margaret Atwood's *The Handmaid's Tale* (1985), but it is worth remembering that there are other books which could also be considered or brought in as background material, for example Wells's science fiction stories *The Time Machine* and *The Island of Doctor Moreau*, which also explore the mutability of human nature, and utopias such as the feminist *Herland* by Charlotte Perkins Gilman (1915) and the behaviourist *Walden Two* by B. F. Skinner (1948). Huxley's own utopia *Island* (1962) is especially interesting, because it presents as positive many features which are presented negatively in *Brave New World*. Eugenic breeding, indoctrination, sleep-teaching, drug use, sexual freedom, a religion without a god and even the custom of showing death to children are among the shared features. All these are developed very differently in *Island*, but their reappearance suggests that Huxley did believe them to be rational ways of dealing with human existence and that in *Brave New World* he was arguing with his own ideas quite as much as others'. In undertaking any comparison between *Brave New World* and other books, it is important to remember that it is not enough simply to list similarities of content. Although these are important, works of fiction cannot be appreciated without consideration of their literary qualities: **characterisation**, narrative techniques, **symbols**, style and so on.

CHECK THE BOOK

Huxley's *Island* is a kind of companion piece to *Brave New World*, showing in contrast what an ideal society might be like.

PART FOUR

CRITICAL HISTORY

EARLY RECEPTION

Many reviewers greeted *Brave New World* as a frivolous piece of entertainment or, if they accepted that it did have deeper intentions, a perverse attack on the forces of progress. Rebecca West, however, perceived it to be 'a serious religious work' informed by science and modern thought. Several of these early responses, including West's, are reprinted in *Aldous Huxley: The Critical Heritage*, edited by Donald Watt (Routledge and Kegan Paul, 1975). Despite the reservations of critics, British readers bought twenty-three thousand copies of the book in two years, and it was soon well on the way to becoming Huxley's best-known work. Some opponents have continued to argue, however, that the book is a superficial, backward-looking one which fails to deal adequately with its subject matter. For example, John Huntington in *The Logic and Fantasy of H. G. Wells and Science Fiction* (Columbia University Press, 1982) complains that the book operates by 'simple plus-minus oppositions' and John Carey in *The Intellectuals and the Masses: Pride and Prejudice Among the Literary Intelligentsia, 1800–1939* (Faber, 1992) sees it as a poorly contrived 'denunciation of mass culture'.

QUESTION

Do you think that the passage of time has made the novel dated, irrelevant or obsolete, or does it still have something to say to us today?

THE 1950S ONWARDS

From the 1950s onwards, several full-length studies of Huxley's work have tried to achieve a deeper appreciation of *Brave New World* by relating it to themes and **plot** devices which are common to his writing as a whole. For example, Jerome Meckier in *Aldous Huxley: Satire and Structure* (Chatto & Windus, 1969) argues that all Huxley's novels depict characters who have very limited, partial views and, by juxtaposing these, he is able to imply the possibility of a greater, more integrated perspective on modern life. Going one step further, *Brave New World* shows a world where, in a misconceived attempt to perfect society, all individuals' outlooks have been deliberately limited with disastrous results. Keith M. May in *Aldous Huxley* (Elek, 1972) examines in detail how the book is structured, both to equip the reader with necessary information and to develop its themes. Robert S. Baker in *The Dark Historic Page: History and Historicism in Aldous Huxley's Social Satire, 1921–39* (University of Wisconsin Press, 1982) considers the features of the World State in the light of Huxley's views about history and social ideals. A number of worthwhile discussions of *Brave New World* are collected in Jerome Meckier, ed., *Critical Essays on Aldous Huxley* (Prentice-Hall, 1996). For an interesting general interview with Huxley, see George Plimpton, ed., *Writers at Work: Second Series* (Secker & Warburg, 1963). There is a thorough overview of his life and work in Jerry W. Carlson's article 'Aldous Huxley' in the *Dictionary of Literary Biography*, Vol. 36 (Gale, 1985).

Several **intertextual** studies have attempted to enhance understanding of the book by placing it in relation to other works, mostly **utopias** and **dystopias**, so that it is seen not simply as an expression of Huxley's views but as a contribution to an ongoing debate about the nature and direction of modern society. Among the most informative of these, from a literary and a political standpoint respectively, are Mark R. Hillegas's *The Future as Nightmare: H. G. Wells and the Anti-Utopians* (Oxford University Press, 1967) and Krishan Kumar's *Utopia and Anti-Utopia in Modern Times* (Blackwell, 1987). Jenni Calder's *Aldous Huxley and George Orwell: Brave New World and Nineteen Eighty-Four* (Arnold, 1976) focuses on the two texts named. Peter Firchow's *The End of Utopia: A Study of Aldous Huxley's Brave New World* (Associated University Presses, 1984) is a wide-ranging discussion of sources and contexts.

Recent **feminist critics**, concerned with attitudes towards gender, particularly in the kind of value placed on women in literature, have questioned the assumptions of male dominance in *Brave New World*. Jane Deery in 'Technology and Gender in Aldous Huxley's Alternative (?) Worlds' (1992, collected in Meckier, 1996) points out that, although the women in the book may in some senses lead more 'liberated' lives than those in 1930s Britain, they are still very much subordinate to men. A similar view is put forward in Deanna

? QUESTION

To what extent would you agree that the representation of women in the book is **stereotypical** and, if this is the case, does it damage the novel in any way?

Madden's article, 'Women in Dystopia', in Katherine Anne Ackley, ed., *Misogyny in Literature: An Essay Collection* (Garland, 1992).

Krishan Kumar (Kumar, 1987) points out that some readers today react to the book with an **oppositional reading**, finding its characters' freedom to enjoy sex and drugs attractive rather than repulsive, and he cites an article by Elaine Baruch, '"A Natural and Necessary Monster": Women in Utopia' (1979), which suggests that the sexual attitudes of Huxley's characters are actually healthier than those of the author. Theodor Adorno in his essay 'Aldous Huxley and Utopia' (cited in Huntington, 1982) offers a Freudian reading of John, claiming that he is not a heroic rebel but a repressed homosexual manifesting neurotic aggression towards Lenina. No doubt Huxley would have taken such responses as evidence that his fears for the future were well founded.

QUESTION

Which aspects of the novel would make it difficult to film? How does Michael R. Joyce deal with them in his 1998 adaptation for the screen?

PART FIVE

BACKGROUND

ALDOUS HUXLEY'S LIFE AND WORK

 CHECK THE NET
There are many useful items on Huxley, including biographical material and a discussion board, at **http://www. somaweb.org**

Aldous Huxley was born in 1894 into a family renowned for its contribution to science and literature. He was a grandson of T.H. Huxley, the eminent scientist and teacher who had championed Darwin's theory of evolution and the teaching of science in schools, and he was a great-nephew of the poet and critic Matthew Arnold, who had argued for a counterbalancing emphasis on literature in the curriculum to instil humane values. This double heritage must have encouraged him to bridge the split between the artistic and scientific ways of looking at the world, evident for so much of the twentieth century. One of his brothers, Julian, became a highly distinguished scientist and author. Aldous himself intended to study medicine, but was prevented from doing so by a recurrent eye disease.

In 1908, the year that he went to Eton, his mother died of cancer. This terrible event left its mark on his writings. In *Brave New World*, for example, John experiences dreadful feelings of guilt about his mother's death which no one else can understand. Huxley's eyesight became so poor after the death of his mother that he had to leave school. He persevered with his studies despite his near blindness, learning Braille as an aid, and went on to take a first-class English degree at Balliol College, Oxford. When the Great War broke out in 1914, he tried to enlist but was rejected due to his disability. In the same year his second brother, Trevenen, committed suicide by hanging himself. This shocking occurrence is also echoed in his fiction, for example by the death which concludes *Brave New World*.

After he graduated in 1916, Huxley spent the remainder of the war years doing farm work at Garsington Manor, the country house of Lady Ottoline Morrell, a prominent patron of the arts. He met many well-known people there, including the novelist and poet D.H. Lawrence, whose attacks on the spiritual inadequacy of modern civilisation made a strong impression upon him, and whose letters he later edited, with a perceptive introduction.

Huxley married Maria Nys, a Belgian, in 1919 and, after making an initial reputation as a promising poet, worked on the *Athenaeum* and other magazines. By the early 1920s he had established himself as a novelist and essayist, and had begun to travel widely. The characters in his novels were often based on well-known people he had met. He depicted them arguing about their ideas in a **witty**, sceptical way in which no one finally prevailed, and as a result he gained the reputation of being a highly erudite and cynical young man who held up contemporary culture to ridicule. *Brave New World* was a turning point in disclosing his genuine unhappiness with the direction of civilisation and his longing to find a better way forward. It can fairly be said that before *Brave New World* Huxley was predominantly a **satirist**, mocking the futility of modern civilisation, but that after it he sought to be something of a prophet, offering constructive solutions to humanity's problems.

Like many other people who had initially supported the Great War, he became disillusioned, first by the nature of the war, then by the terms of the peace settlement, and as a result he became a pacifist. His advocacy of non-violence became unacceptable to many of his readers, however, once Germany began to invade other nations and the prospect of a Second World War grew near. It also made his decision to move to California in 1937 a highly controversial one. Huxley seemed to be running away from the enemies of freedom and, worse still, running away to the very place whose mass culture and vulgarity he had so often mocked in his novels and essays. In the USA, despite his professed dislike of both Los Angeles and the cinema (evident in the 'feelies' of *Brave New World*), he lived in Hollywood and tried to make money writing film scripts. He also pursued his interest in mysticism and Hindu teaching, seeking to reconcile the insights of Eastern spiritual thought with Western science, eventually advocating the use of hallucinogenic drugs as a help in attaining enlightenment. His later writings were an important influence on the hippy movement of the 1960s, although it is unlikely that he would have approved of all its features. Huxley died in 1963.

CHECK THE BOOK
To learn more about Huxley read the biographies of his life by Nicholas Murray and David Bradshaw.

OTHER WORKS BY ALDOUS HUXLEY

The **satirical** novels Huxley produced before *Brave New World* are *Crome Yellow* (1921), *Antic Hay* (1923), *Those Barren Leaves*

(1925) and *Point Counter Point* (1928). In Chapters 5 and 22 of *Crome Yellow* a character called Scogan sketches the ideas about the future later developed in *Brave New World*. Huxley's later novels are *Eyeless in Gaza* (1936), *After Many a Summer* (1939), *Time Must Have a Stop* (1944), *Ape and Essence* (1948), *The Genius and the Goddess* (1955) and *Island* (1962). *Island* is a **utopian** novel which depicts Huxley's ideal world, in opposition to the **dystopia** of *Brave New World*. His short stories first appeared in *Limbo* (1920), *Mortal Coils* (1922), *Little Mexican* (1924) and *Brief Candles* (1930), and are also available in his *Collected Short Stories* (1957).

CHECK THE BOOK

Brave New World Revisited is not, as its title seems to promise, a sequel to Huxley's dystopia, but a collection of articles on loosely related topics.

Along with his *Collected Essays* (1959), the chief volumes in which Huxley discussed his ideas are *The Perennial Philosophy* (1946), *The Doors of Perception* (1954), *Heaven and Hell* (1956), *Brave New World Revisited* (1958) and *Literature and Science* (1963). Huxley's other non-fictional works include several travel books, *Grey Eminence* (1941), which is a life of Cardinal Richelieu's adviser, Father Joseph, and *The Devils of Loudun* (1952), a study of sexual hysteria in seventeenth-century France.

SOCIAL BACKGROUND

Huxley came to prominence as a writer in the 1920s, a decade marked by widespread disillusionment with the Great War of 1914–18. Over 8 million people had been killed in the war; more than 13 million if consequences are included such as the Russian Revolution and the epidemics which ravaged Europe in the war's aftermath. This colossal suffering seemed to have achieved very little and, in the eyes of some people, the ideals which politicians and other members of the establishment had used to justify the war therefore became discredited.

It is difficult to generalise about the population as a whole, but there was certainly a significant proportion of the younger generation in many countries who felt disillusioned, cynical and ready to ignore the old-fashioned morality of their elders and embrace new forms of behaviour. Church membership and attendance went into steep decline. Women increasingly smoked and drank in public. European light music was challenged by the exuberant, syncopated sound of American jazz, bringing with it high-tempo dances like the Charleston. In thinking circles, 'Modernist' innovations such as Einstein's theory of relativity, Freudian psychology and Surrealist art called into question notions and customs which had previously been taken for granted. The early fiction of Huxley, like that of other writers of the 'Jazz Age' such as Ernest Hemingway and F. Scott Fitzgerald, holds up for inspection a restless era when right and wrong are in dispute and individuals feel free to pursue their own codes, sometimes with damaging consequences for themselves and others. When *Brave New World* depicts promiscuity, drug-taking and the replacement of religion by frantic partying, Huxley is **satirising** his own period as much as he is predicting the future.

CHECK THE BOOK
Chapter 3 of Malcolm Bradbury's *The Modern English Novel* (1993) gives a social and cultural account of the period.

Some features of life between the world wars are notably absent from *Brave New World*, particularly the collapse of the world economy (in Britain unemployment was running at over fifteen per cent when the book was first published), and, as one consequence of that collapse, the rise of totalitarian states such as Fascist Italy and Nazi Germany. *Brave New World* touches upon such developments only in Mond's brief references to 'the great Economic Collapse' and 'the Nine Years' War' (p. 43) in Chapter 3. Economic collapse and war are the features of the twentieth century that the World State is intended to eliminate; the book's focus is on the price which might have to be paid for their elimination.

CHECK THE NET
There are several relevant essays at **http://www. findarticles.com,** including 'Aldous Huxley's Americanisation of the *Brave New World* Typescript',** which examines how Huxley put references to American culture into the book.

A less obvious, but still notable, feature of the period which is reflected in *Brave New World* is the development of mass culture. 'High' and 'low' cultures remained distinct between the two world wars. Intellectuals of the period might be prepared to admire the folk culture of pre-industrial times, but they were hesitant about finding value in the commercially produced, American-influenced popular culture of their own day. Whereas folk culture was produced by the people for the people, mass entertainment was made by capitalists for profit. Thinkers of left-wing views generally regarded mass culture, therefore, as propaganda and distraction, designed to stimulate false needs and so prevent the common people from thinking and feeling for themselves. Right-wing traditionalists held views which differed from the left's only in emphasis, seeing mass culture as a standardised set of products designed for an unenlightened majority who were incapable of appreciating serious, classic work. Such dismissal is evident in Huxley's depiction of recreational activities in the World State. Games like 'Riemann-surface tennis' and 'Obstacle Golf' satirise the growing popularity of sports such as tennis, golf, soccer, cricket and motoring. The increased circulation of working-class newspapers is mocked in *The Delta Mirror*. Cinema, broadcasting and dance halls are targeted in the 'feelies', 'the Bureaux of Propaganda by Television' and the 'Westminster Abbey Cabaret'

Although Huxley became more open-minded in his later years, his earlier writings have been accused of treating ordinary people in a way that is patronising, **stereotypical** and snobbish, reflecting the class divisions of Britain between the wars. The repeated descriptions of the World State's population as 'maggots' and 'lice', the portrayal of the Deltas as repulsive clones and the dismissal of the Epsilons as ape-like morons may be intended as a warning **caricature** of how mass society could degrade human beings, but these passages can also be interpreted as evidence of an underlying contempt for ordinary people. In Chapter 7 of *Island*, the **utopian** novel which Huxley produced near the end of his life, as a kind of 'answer' to *Brave New World*, the perception of other people as maggots is treated as a symptom of cynicism and lovelessness, revealing more about the beholder than about those he sees.

QUESTION

To what extent does the depiction of lower-class people – the Deltas and Epsilons – present a problem for the modern reader?

LITERARY BACKGROUND

What kind of book is *Brave New World*? A '**satirical dystopian science fiction novel of ideas**' might be an accurate classification, but is obviously one which is too unwieldy to be helpful. The elements of the definition need to be broken down and considered one at a time if we are to understand what Huxley was seeking to achieve.

Ever since Plato's *Republic* in the third century BC, writers have been inventing imaginary societies as a way of holding up an ideal of what the world should be like and challenging their readers' assumptions about the customs and institutions of their day. The most famous book of this type is *Utopia* by Thomas More (1516) and, because of this, all such imaginary societies are now called utopias. The name is a play on two Greek words, 'eu-topos', meaning 'good place', and 'ou-topos', 'no place'. Both parts of the pun are significant. A utopia is rarely intended to be a practical proposal, since any utopian book which is simply a plan for a new society is bound to become obsolete as social conditions and people's ideas change. Utopias which remain worth reading are ones which mix idealism and social criticism with imagination for its own sake and which present their ideas in a way that is enjoyable to read. They incorporate not only a story and characters of the sort we expect to find in fiction, but lengthy conversations about customs, sustained descriptions such as we might associate with a travel book, and essay-like passages of opinion and discussion.

CHECK THE BOOK
Krishan Kumar's *Utopia and Anti-Utopia in Modern Times* (1987) is an informative study of imaginary societies.

The modern utopian tradition dates from *Looking Backward: 2000–1887* by the American reformer Edward Bellamy, first published in 1888. A huge bestseller, this book led to the setting up of clubs, journals and even a political party. The English socialist and designer William Morris, who objected to the urban and highly regulated nature of Bellamy's utopia, retaliated with a utopia of his own, *News from Nowhere* (1890), depicting a non-industrial ideal world. Ever since, authors have offered their public a variety of utopias, responding both to the ideas of their predecessors and to new social change. The most notable utopian of the first half of the twentieth century was H. G. Wells.

The utopian tradition also includes what have come to be called dystopias, portraits of imaginary societies which are worse than our own, intended to dramatise unhealthy values and trends in the present and warn against future developments. Wells was unusual in producing books of both kinds, and his dystopian works have been even more influential on later writers than his utopian ones. Utopias and dystopias are not in fact entirely distinct types of book, since it only takes the reader's disagreement with the author to convert one to the other, and some of the best productions in this field have been portrayals of societies which are not so much better or worse than ours as challengingly different. Perhaps the greatest book of this kind is Jonathan Swift's *Gulliver's Travels* (1726), which entertainingly recounts Gulliver's visits to several curious lands, but finally leaves him disillusioned with human nature. Later examples are *Erewhon* (1872) by Samuel Butler and Wells's *The First Men in the Moon* (1901).

 CHECK THE BOOK
Yevgeny Zamyatin's *We* is one of the greatest dystopias, and provided the basic storyline for George Orwell's *Nineteen Eighty-Four*.

Science fiction with a utopian or dystopian element tends to differ from more wholeheartedly utopian and dystopian writing by presenting social change as largely the result of scientific developments and placing greater emphasis on storytelling, not in order to downplay ideas about society but in order to subordinate them to the characters' adventures. Along with Wells's *Time Machine* (1895), *We* (1920) by Yevgeny Zamyatin and *Nineteen Eighty-Four* (1949) by George Orwell, *Brave New World* is one of the most memorable examples of dystopian science fiction. It shows a world which has developed from our own due to scientific developments: first in warfare, creating global conflict; then in social conditioning, making possible a stable world state. It presents that world through the adventures of a handful of characters, with shifting emphasis between character and discussion as the story progresses. It implies social criticisms about the present and speculates about the future, but has enough narrative interest and imaginative development to hold the attention even of a reader who is unconcerned about the book's 'message'.

There is another distinct tradition to which *Brave New World* belongs, however, which is the 'novel of ideas'. This is a type of fiction in which action is less important than explicit discussion between the characters. Although it does sometimes deal in fantastic events, it does not usually feature radical transformations of society like the types of books discussed previously. Huxley's novels of the 1920s which made his reputation are often classified as novels of ideas. The title of one of them, *Point Counter Point*, indicates clearly that its interest lies not so much in the outcome of the story as in the debates in which the characters engage, one point balanced against another. This approach is continued in *Brave New World*. Chapters 16 and 17 consist entirely of conversation, for example, and the book never arrives at a definite conclusion to its arguments, leaving the readers to draw his or her own.

The best-known English 'novelist of ideas' is Thomas Love
Peacock, whose work Wells and Huxley both admired, and the best
known of all such writers is the French author Voltaire. It is likely
that Voltaire's *Candide* (1758) had some influence on *Brave New
World*. Like Candide, John is a naive central character who lives
through a series of fantastic events, which, together with his
reflections upon them, helps us to think about current moral and
political issues.

**CHECK
THE BOOK**

Voltaire's *Candide* is
a brief, entertaining
and highly
influential satire.

Both Voltaire and Peacock were satirists who did not just offer their
readers a discussion of ideas, but presented the ideas with comic
vigour, sometimes resorting to violent **slapstick** action in order to
mock human folly and evil. By the end of Chapter 2 of *Candide*,
the hero has already received four hundred strokes of the whip,
exposing every nerve in his back, and has only just escaped
beheading. In Chapter 8 of Peacock's *Crotchet Castle* (1831), the
Reverend Doctor Folliott violently beats off two muggers, one of
whom accidentally shoots the other in the head, before himself
toppling headfirst into a thicket of nettles.

This kind of action, which today we might associate with animated
cartoons more readily than with social thought, is also present in
Brave New World: for example in Chapter 13 when Lenina,
distracted by her love for John, fails to immunise an embryo
('Twenty-two years eight months and four days from that moment,
a promising young Alpha-Minus … was to die of trypanosomiasis',
p. 170), and on several occasions in the book when John whips
himself while cursing in Shakespearean English. Such moments of
apparently flippant, cartoon-like violence caused some of Huxley's
early readers to overlook the real yearning for spiritual and
philosophical enlightenment which lay beneath his derisive humour.
If we are aware of the kind of book he is writing, however, we can
at least consider that his humour and his seriousness may be
compatible. Similarly, an awareness that the book is a science fiction
dystopia, rather than a realistic novel, may make us willing to forgo
depth of **characterisation** and subtlety of **plot** in return for
exuberance of imagination and the witty presentation of important
ideas.

SCIENTIFIC BACKGROUND

EUGENICS

When *Brave New World* was written in the early 1930s, there was widespread enthusiasm for 'eugenics': the scientific planning of human breeding to improve the health of future generations. Unfortunately, research into the subject was often crude and unreliable, and it was not possible to use eugenics in a positive way, to assist in the creation of healthier people, only negatively, to prevent the breeding of those who were judged by other people in authority to be inferior. Those targeted included alcoholics, epileptics, criminals, people with mental disabilities, and even members of racial minorities. In *The Science of Life* (1930), a major introduction to biology written by H. G. Wells, his son G. P. Wells and Aldous's brother, Julian Huxley, published shortly before *Brave New World*, the sterilisation of thousands of 'mental defectives' in the USA is praised. The authors, representing enlightened, progressive views of the period, firmly oppose 'harshness or brutality' in the implementation of negative eugenics, and they caution against judging people 'unfit' simply by reason of their social class, but they accept that there is probably a lower-class group who represent 'pockets of evil germ plasm' and who might be 'bribed or otherwise persuaded to accept voluntary sterilisation'.

Today people have become cautious about holding and expressing such views. This is partly due to increased understanding of the complexity of the scientific issues, but perhaps to an even greater extent due to the example of Nazi Germany in the 1930s and 1940s. The Nazis sterilised four hundred thousand people, then, supported by bogus research into racial characteristics, began a programme of exterminating those they considered to be members of 'inferior', non-Aryan races, such as Jews. News of these genocidal crimes largely discredited negative eugenics as a theory, although this does not mean that its practice went away completely. The US state of Virginia continued to sterilise mentally disabled people into the 1970s. It is still common throughout the world to check embryos for Down's Syndrome and abort some of those which fail the test, and in some cultures to test unofficially for gender and abort unwanted girls.

 CHECK THE BOOK
Matt Ridley's *Genome: Autobiography of a Species in 23 Chapters* (1999) is an accessible introduction to the topic of genes and genetic modification.

Brave New World's contribution to the eugenics debate of the 1930s was to offer a plausible account of positive eugenics, depicting a system in which human characteristics can be chosen in advance. The descriptions of how this is done use enough scientific terminology to seem plausible, but as Huxley notes in his 1946 Foreword, the science of the first half of the twentieth century was insufficiently developed to carry out such a scheme in practice. He suggests in the Foreword that 'a foolproof system of eugenics' is a project which will take centuries to complete.

However, Huxley's ideas about producing specific types of people and controlling their development no longer seem so far-fetched as they once did, for in 1953 it was discovered that the genetic 'recipe' for the construction of living creatures is carried by the chemical DNA, contained in each body cell, and by the end of the twentieth century it had become practicable to modify that recipe. A cell contains two slightly different sets of instructions, one contributed by the mother, one by the father, recorded on spiral-shaped molecules of DNA called chromosomes. Human beings have twenty-three chromosomes, each of which carries several thousand separate instructions called genes. Scientists have already identified particular genes which control particular characteristics and, in some cases, can trigger physical defects. For example, the fatal illness Huntington's chorea is caused by a mutation in one gene on chromosome 4. Just as it is possible to modify crops genetically in order to make them resistant to parasites, so it should be possible to modify human beings to 'weed out' diseases and unwanted characteristics.

The contraceptive pill, organ transplants and human eggs fertilised outside the body have demonstrated that it is increasingly possible for the human race to exercise choice about its development as a species. Some scientists are now predicting that, thanks to genetic engineering, before the twenty-first century has run its course sex will become a purely recreational activity and reproduction a purely clinical one, with fertilisation of eggs inside the laboratory permitting some degree of design of human characteristics. The latter might begin negatively with the screening out of genetic defects, then extend to positive choices about appearance and even personality.

 CHECK THE NET
Find articles and resources on all aspects of genetic modification, cloning and the US Human Genome Project, at **http://www. doegenomes.org**

In practice the 'editing' and 'correcting' of human beings is an extremely complex task. There are no single genes which control intelligence or criminal tendencies, and which can be modified to make us all law-abiding geniuses. On the contrary, human behaviour develops through the interaction of genes with each other and with the person's experiences and environment, in ways so elaborate as to be beyond prediction.

Nonetheless, the prospect of modifying human character before birth has led to renewed interest in *Brave New World*, the one classic work of fiction which addresses this topic and considers the important issues it entails. Who should have control over what can be done to embryos? Who is to say what is an improvement in 'fitness' and what a monstrosity? How far should genetic decisions be made in the interests of individuals or of the community? How can we safeguard against accidents such as the creation of new diseases? And will new social classes emerge, of genetic haves and have-nots with new customs and new mentalities? Huxley's cautionary tale has naturally been cited by many writers who tackle the subject. One book published in 1999 was even named *Brave New Worlds* and included a chapter called 'The Right to be Unhappy' after Mond's phrase in Chapter 17 (p. 219).

CHECK THE FILM
Some of these issues receive a thoughtful presentation in Andrew Niccol's 1997 science fiction film *Gattaca*.

World events	Aldous Huxley's life	Literary events
		1516 Thomas More, *Utopia*
		1726 Jonathan Swift, *Gulliver's Travels*
		1755 Jean-Jacques Rousseau and the 'Noble Savage'
		1758 Voltaire, *Candide*
1797 Immanuel Kant's 'categorical imperative'		
		1817 Thomas Love Peacock, *Melincourt*
		1833 Alfred Tennyson, 'St Simeon Stylites'
1848 Karl Marx, *Communist Manifesto*		
1859 Charles Darwin, *On the Origin of Species*		
		1872 Samuel Butler, *Erewhon*
		1880 Fyodor Dostoevsky, *The Brothers Karamazov*
	1887 Julian, brother, born	
	1888 Matthew Arnold, great-uncle, dies	**1888** Edward Bellamy, *Looking Backward: 2000–1887*
1890s Sigmund Freud develops psychoanalysis		**1890** William Morris, *News from Nowhere*
1893 T. H. Huxley, *Evolution and Ethics*		
	1894 Aldous Leonard Huxley born	
	1895 T. H. Huxley, grandfather, dies	**1895** H. G. Wells, *The Time Machine*
		1896 H. G. Wells, *The Island of Doctor Moreau*
		1899 H. G. Wells, *When the Sleeper Wakes*
		1901 H. G. Wells, *The First Men in the Moon*
		1905 H. G. Wells, *A Modern Utopia;* George Bernard Shaw, *Man and Superman*

World events	Aldous Huxley's life	Literary events
1907 Henry Deterding founds Shell; first synthetic plastic; Ivan Pavlov, *Conditioned Reflexes*		
1908 Ford Model T car; first assembly line	**1908–11** At Eton **1908** Julia, mother, dies of cancer	**1908** E. M. Forster, *A Room with a View*
1909 English Channel crossed by monoplane		
	1910 Becomes almost blind with eye infection	
1912 First Keystone film comedy		
1913 Igor Stravinsky, *Rite of Spring*		
1914 Outbreak of First World War	**1914** Tries to enlist but is rejected; brother, Trevenen, hangs himself	
1915 D. W. Griffith, *Birth of a Nation*		**1915** Charlotte Perkins Gilman, *Herland*
	1916 Gains first at Balliol College, Oxford	**1916** Franz Kafka, *Metamorphosis*
	1916–17 Does farm work at Garsington Manor; meets D. H. Lawrence, Bertrand Russell, Mark Gertler, Clive Bell	
	1916–20 Four collections of poetry	
1917 Russian Revolution	**1917** Half-brother, Andrew, born	
1918 First World War ends; votes for women	**1917–19** Teaches at Eton	
	1919 Marries Maria Nys; writes for *Athenaeum*	
1920 First radio stations	**1920** *Limbo* (short stories)	**1920** Yevgeny Zamyatin, *We*
1920–33 Prohibition of alcohol, USA		
1921 London's first birth control clinic	**1921** *Crome Yellow*	**1921** John Dos Passos, *Three Soldiers*
1922 Mussolini comes to power in Italy; inauguration of USSR	**1922** *Mortal Coils*	**1922** T. S. Eliot, *The Waste Land*; F. Scott Fitzgerald, *Tales of the Jazz Age*; James Joyce, *Ulysses*; Sinclair Lewis, *Babbitt*
	1923 Moves to Italy; *Antic Hay*	**1923** H. G. Wells, *Men Like Gods*

World events	Aldous Huxley's life	Literary events
1924 Lenin dies		**1924** André Breton, *Surrealist Manifesto*
1925 Adolf Hitler, *Mein Kampf*; John B. Watson, *Behaviorism*	**1925** *Those Barren Leaves*	**1925** Mikhail Bulgakov, *The White Guard*
		1926 Ernest Hemingway, *The Sun Also Rises*
		1927 D. H. Lawrence, *Mornings in Mexico*; Virginia Woolf, *To the Lighthouse*
1928 Alfred Mund co-founds ICI; Margaret Mead, *Coming of Age in Samoa*	**1928** *Point Counter Point*	
1929 Wall Street Crash; Great Depression; Movietone Newsreels begin		**1929** William Faulkner, *The Sound and the Fury*
1930 H. G. and G. P. Wells and Julian Huxley, *The Science of Life*	**1930** Moves to Côte d'Azur	**1930** Evelyn Waugh, *Vile Bodies*
1932 British Union of Fascists launched	**1932** *Brave New World*	**1932** Stella Gibbons, *Cold Comfort Farm*
1933 Hitler German chancellor		
1936 Charlie Chaplin, *Modern Times*; first TV service launched by BBC	**1936** *Eyeless in Gaza*	
	1937 Moves to California	
	1939 *After Many a Summer*	
	1946 *The Perennial Philosophy*	
		1948 B. F. Skinner, *Walden Two*
		1949 George Orwell, *Nineteen Eighty-Four*
	1952 *The Devils of Loudun*	
	1954 *The Doors of Perception*	
	1955 Wife Maria dies	
	1956 *Heaven and Hell*; marries Laura Archera	
	1958 *Brave New World Revisited*	
	1962 *Island*	
	1963 *Literature and Science*; dies, author of more than 50 books	
		1985 Margaret Atwood, *The Handmaid's Tale*

Katherine Anne Ackley, ed., *Misogyny in Literature: An Essay Collection*, Garland, 1992
For a feminist viewpoint on *Brave New World*, see Deanna Madden's article 'Women in Dystopia'

Robert S. Baker, *The Dark Historic Page: History and Historicism in Aldous Huxley's Social Satire, 1921–39*, University of Wisconsin Press, 1982

Jenni Calder, *Aldous Huxley and George Orwell: Brave New World and Nineteen Eighty-Four*, Arnold, 1976

John Carey, *The Intellectuals and the Masses: Pride and Prejudice Among the Literary Intelligentsia, 1800–1939*, Faber, 1992

Jerry W. Carlson, 'Aldous Huxley' in *Dictionary of Literary Biography*, Vol. 36, Gale, 1985

Peter Firchow, *The End of Utopia: A Study of Aldous Huxley's Brave New World*, Associated University Presses, 1984

Mark R. Hillegas, *The Future as Nightmare: H. G. Wells and the Anti-Utopians*, Oxford University Press, 1967

John Huntington, *The Logic and Fantasy of H. G. Wells and Science Fiction*, Columbia University Press, 1982

Krishan Kumar, *Utopia and Anti-Utopia in Modern Times*, Blackwell Publishers, 1987

Keith M. May, *Aldous Huxley*, Elek, 1972

Jerome Meckier, *Aldous Huxley: Satire and Structure*, Chatto & Windus, 1969

Jerome Meckier, *Critical Essays on Aldous Huxley*, Prentice-Hall, 1996
A number of worthwhile discussions are collected here, including Jane Deery's 'Technology and Gender in Aldous Huxley's Alternative (?) Worlds'

Nicholas Murray, *Aldous Huxley: An English Intellectual*, Little, Brown, 2002

George Plimpton, ed., *Writers at Work: Second Series*, Secker & Warburg, 1963

Donald Watt, ed., *Aldous Huxley: The Critical Heritage*, Routledge and Kegan Paul, 1975

GENERAL READING

Malcolm Bradbury, *The Modern English Novel*, Secker & Warburg, 1993
Chapter 3 gives a social and cultural account of the period

Dennis Freeborn, *Style: Text Analysis and Linguistic Criticism*, Macmillan, 1996

Eric Hobsbawm, *Age of Extremes: The Short Twentieth Century, 1914–1991*, Michael Joseph, 1994

Mark Holloway, *Heavens on Earth: Utopian Communities in America, 1680–1880*, Dover Publications, 1966

Jonathan Howard, *Darwin: A Very Short Introduction*, Oxford University Press, 1982

Michael McKeon, ed., *Theory of the Novel: A Historical Approach*, Johns Hopkins University Press, 2000

Mark Mazower, *Dark Continent: Europe's Twentieth Century*, Penguin, 1998

Martin Montgomery, Alan Durant, Nigel Fabb, Tom Furniss and Sarah Mills, *Ways of Reading: Advanced Reading Skills for Students of English Literature*, Routledge, 1992

Matt Ridley, *Genome: Autobiography of a Species in 23 Chapters*, Fourth Estate, 1999

Peter Singer, *Marx: A Very Short Introduction*, Oxford University Press, 1980

Anthony Storr, *Freud: A Very Short Introduction*, Oxford University Press, 1989

Richard Webster, *Why Freud Was Wrong: Sin, Science and Psychoanalysis*, HarperCollins, 1995

LITERARY TERMS

allusion, allusive (from Latin, 'to touch lightly upon') a passing reference in a work of literature to something outside itself

burlesque (from Italian, 'ridicule') dealing with a subject in a deliberately incongruous style

caricature (from Italian, 'to exaggerate') a ludicrous rendering of character, achieved by the exaggeration of appearance or behaviour

characterisation the way in which a writer creates characters so as to convey their personalities effectively, attract or repel our sympathies and integrate their behaviour into the story

comic relief the inclusion of a comic scene in a narrative for the purpose of dramatic contrast with more serious episodes

distance, distancing a work of literature should arouse its reader's sympathies, but if a reader identifies too strongly with a character, situation or idea, whether for emotional, personal or political reasons, it may distort judgement. A writer may therefore create 'distance' between the reader and the events of the text, for example by commenting on the action or by giving an otherwise heroic character unsympathetic faults

dystopia an imaginary world which is worse than our own, the opposite of a **utopia**

ellipsis (from Greek, 'leaving out') the omission of one or more words from a sentence for reasons of economy or style: 'Told them of the *corpus luteum* extract' (Chapter 1, p. 9; this example omits the subject, 'he')

epigraph a quotation placed at the beginning of a literary work as a clue or hint concerning its meaning

farce, farcical a kind of drama intended primarily to provoke laughter, using exaggerated characters and complicated **plots**, full of absurd episodes, ludicrous situations and knockabout action. Sexual escapades and mistaken identity are frequent elements in the plot

feminist criticism seeks to explore the masculine bias in texts and challenge traditional ideas about them, constructing and then offering a feminine perspective on works of art

foil a character who illuminates by contrast some aspects of a more central character

free indirect discourse a technique of narrating the thoughts or speech of a character by incorporating their words or ideas into a third-person narrative: 'His hand dropped back. How beautiful she was! How beautiful' (Chapter 9, p. 13)

image, imagery in its narrowest sense, an image is a word-picture, describing some visible scene or object, such as the description of the Park Lane Hospital at the beginning of Chapter 14. More commonly, imagery refers to the figurative language (**similes** and **metaphors**) in a work of literature: 'The mesa was like a ship becalmed in a strait of lion-coloured dust' (Chapter 7, p. 96)

intertextuality a term referring to the many kinds of relationships that exist between texts, such as adaptation, translation, imitation, **allusion**, plagiarism and **parody**

irony, ironic saying one thing while meaning another, with the true meaning to some extent contradicting the surface one. **Sarcasm** is a comparatively straightforward type, when someone makes a mocking statement which in the given context clearly means the reverse of what it says. (In Chapter 1 the motto of the World State, 'COMMUNITY, IDENTITY, STABILITY', is sarcastically described as 'Grand words' and, even more clearly, we hear of 'Independent existence – so called'.) More sophisticated irony can be much harder to recognise and interpret, however, because it relies on the writer and reader sharing values and knowledge. A highly ironic piece of writing may even suggest several different ways of responding to statements, characters and events, and conceal entirely the attitudes of its author

metaphor goes further than a comparison between two different things or ideas by fusing them together: one thing is described as being another thing, carrying over its associations: 'The light was frozen, dead, a ghost' (Chapter 1, p. 1)

minor sentence a group of words punctuated like a sentence and functioning as a similar unit of meaning, but lacking the grammatical constituents of a full sentence: 'A squat grey building of only thirty-four storeys' (Chapter 1, p. 1; this example omits the subject and verb 'it was')

novel of ideas a type of narrative fiction in which action is less important than explicit discussion between the characters

onomatopoeia words which sound like the noise which they describe: 'the *buzzing* was interrupted by a stethoscopic wheeze and crackle, by hiccoughs and sudden *squeaks*' (Chapter 18, p. 277; my italics)

oppositional reading an interpretation of a work of literature which consciously goes against its author's apparent intention

parable a narrative which demonstrates a moral or a lesson

parenthesis material inserted into a passage (usually to qualify, clarify or explain) which grammatically is not part of the original construction and so is commonly marked out by brackets or dashes

parody an imitation of something, for example a style of writing or a particular work of literature, intended to ridicule its characteristic features

plot the plan of a literary work. More than the simple sequence of events, 'plot' suggests a pattern of relationships between events: a story with a beginning, middle and end, with its various parts bound together by cause and effect, exhibiting a version of typical experience or a view of morality. Suspense is vital to make a plot entertaining: we should be made to want to know what is going to happen, and be surprised by new incidents, yet be satisfied that they grow logically out of what we already know

sarcasm see **irony**

satire literature which exhibits and examines vice and folly and makes them appear ridiculous or contemptible. Satire differs from straightforward comedy in having a purpose, using laughter to attack its objects

science fiction literature about imaginary marvels or disasters created by future scientific discoveries and technological developments

simile an explicit comparison in which one thing is said to be like another. Similes always contain the words 'like' or 'as': 'The sexophones wailed like melodious cats' (Chapter 5, section 1, p. 67)

slapstick broad comedy with knockabout action, fighting, clowning and so on

stereotype, stereotypical something which conforms to a standard, fixed idea. The word can be used pejoratively, to indicate an ordinary, commonplace perception which has been made dull by frequent repetition, a person or event so ordinary that it conforms to such an expectation, or a prejudiced view of someone which falsely assumes that they fit the expectation. The word may also be used neutrally, to signify stock characters, ideas and situations which are the typical material of literature

stream of consciousness the attempt to convey all that is passing through a character's mind by recording it as it passes: 'He was empty. Empty, and cold, and rather sick, and giddy. He leaned against the wall to steady himself. Remorseless, treacherous, lecherous ...' (Chapter 8, p. 120)

symbol, symbolic something which represents something else (often an idea or quality) either by analogy or association. Many symbols exist by convention or tradition. Sunlight, for example, is a positive image, suggesting vitality, pleasure and naturalness (shut out from the Hatchery in Chapter 1, shining on the babies all too briefly in Chapter 2)

tragedy, tragic a story which traces the downfall of an individual, and shows in so doing both the capacities and the limitations of human life

utopia an imaginary world which is better than our own

wit combining or contrasting ideas and expressions in an unexpected and intellectually pleasing manner

Michael Sherborne is Curriculum Manager of English and Humanities at Luton Sixth Form College. He is the author of the York Notes Advanced on *A Midsummer Night's Dream* and *Nineteen Eighty-Four*. He has edited *The Country of the Blind and Other Stories by H. G. Wells* (Oxford University Press, 1996, not available in the EC) and – under the name, Michael Draper – has written *Modern Novelists: H. G. Wells* (Macmillan/St Martin's Press, 1987).

General editor

Martin Gray, former Head of the Department of English Studies at the University of Stirling, and of Literary Studies at the University of Luton

NOTES

Maya Angelou
I Know Why the Caged Bird Sings

Jane Austen
Pride and Prejudice

Alan Ayckbourn
Absent Friends

Elizabeth Barrett Browning
Selected Poems

Robert Bolt
A Man for All Seasons

Harold Brighouse
Hobson's Choice

Charlotte Brontë
Jane Eyre

Emily Brontë
Wuthering Heights

Shelagh Delaney
A Taste of Honey

Charles Dickens
David Copperfield
Great Expectations
Hard Times
Oliver Twist

Roddy Doyle
Paddy Clarke Ha Ha Ha

George Eliot
Silas Marner
The Mill on the Floss

Anne Frank
The Diary of a Young Girl

William Golding
Lord of the Flies

Oliver Goldsmith
She Stoops to Conquer

Willis Hall
The Long and the Short and the Tall

Thomas Hardy
Far from the Madding Crowd
The Mayor of Casterbridge
Tess of the d'Urbervilles
The Withered Arm and other Wessex Tales

L.P. Hartley
The Go-Between

Seamus Heaney
Selected Poems

Susan Hill
I'm the King of the Castle

Barry Hines
A Kestrel for a Knave

Louise Lawrence
Children of the Dust

Harper Lee
To Kill a Mockingbird

Laurie Lee
Cider with Rosie

Arthur Miller
The Crucible
A View from the Bridge

Robert O'Brien
Z for Zachariah

Frank O'Connor
My Oedipus Complex and Other Stories

George Orwell
Animal Farm

J.B. Priestley
An Inspector Calls
When We Are Married

Willy Russell
Educating Rita
Our Day Out

J.D. Salinger
The Catcher in the Rye

William Shakespeare
Henry IV Part I
Henry V
Julius Caesar
Macbeth
The Merchant of Venice
A Midsummer Night's Dream
Much Ado About Nothing

Romeo and Juliet
The Tempest
Twelfth Night

George Bernard Shaw
Pygmalion

Mary Shelley
Frankenstein

R.C. Sherriff
Journey's End

Rukshana Smith
Salt on the snow

John Steinbeck
Of Mice and Men

Robert Louis Stevenson
Dr Jekyll and Mr Hyde

Jonathan Swift
Gulliver's Travels

Robert Swindells
Daz 4 Zoe

Mildred D. Taylor
Roll of Thunder, Hear My Cry

Mark Twain
Huckleberry Finn

James Watson
Talking in Whispers

Edith Wharton
Ethan Frome

William Wordsworth
Selected Poems

A Choice of Poets

Mystery Stories of the Nineteenth Century including The Signalman

Nineteenth Century Short Stories

Poetry of the First World War

Six Women Poets

For the AQA Anthology:
Duffy and Armitage & Pre-1914 Poetry

Heaney and Clarke & Pre-1914 Poetry

Poems from Different Cultures

Margaret Atwood
Cat's Eye
The Handmaid's Tale

Jane Austen
Emma
Mansfield Park
Persuasion
Pride and Prejudice
Sense and Sensibility

Alan Bennett
Talking Heads

William Blake
Songs of Innocence and of Experience

Charlotte Brontë
Jane Eyre
Villette

Emily Brontë
Wuthering Heights

Angela Carter
Nights at the Circus

Geoffrey Chaucer
The Franklin's Prologue and Tale
The Merchant's Prologue and Tale
The Miller's Prologue and Tale
The Prologue to the Canterbury Tales
The Wife of Bath's Prologue and Tale

Samuel Coleridge
Selected Poems

Joseph Conrad
Heart of Darkness

Daniel Defoe
Moll Flanders

Charles Dickens
Bleak House
Great Expectations
Hard Times

Emily Dickinson
Selected Poems

John Donne
Selected Poems

Carol Ann Duffy
Selected Poems

George Eliot
Middlemarch
The Mill on the Floss

T.S. Eliot
Selected Poems
The Waste Land

F. Scott Fitzgerald
The Great Gatsby

E.M. Forster
A Passage to India

Brian Friel
Translations

Thomas Hardy
Jude the Obscure
The Mayor of Casterbridge
The Return of the Native
Selected Poems
Tess of the d'Urbervilles

Seamus Heaney
Selected Poems from 'Opened Ground'

Nathaniel Hawthorne
The Scarlet Letter

Homer
The Iliad
The Odyssey

Aldous Huxley
Brave New World

Kazuo Ishiguro
The Remains of the Day

Ben Jonson
The Alchemist

James Joyce
Dubliners

John Keats
Selected Poems

Philip Larkin
The Whitsun Weddings and Selected Poems

Christopher Marlowe
Doctor Faustus
Edward II

Arthur Miller
Death of a Salesman

John Milton
Paradise Lost Books I & II

Toni Morrison
Beloved

George Orwell
Nineteen Eighty-Four

Sylvia Plath
Selected Poems

Alexander Pope
Rape of the Lock & Selected Poems

William Shakespeare
Antony and Cleopatra
As You Like It
Hamlet
Henry IV Part I
King Lear
Macbeth
Measure for Measure
The Merchant of Venice
A Midsummer Night's Dream
Much Ado About Nothing
Othello
Richard II
Richard III
Romeo and Juliet
The Taming of the Shrew
The Tempest
Twelfth Night
The Winter's Tale

George Bernard Shaw
Saint Joan

Mary Shelley
Frankenstein

Jonathan Swift
Gulliver's Travels and A Modest Proposal

Alfred Tennyson
Selected Poems

Virgil
The Aeneid

Alice Walker
The Color Purple

Oscar Wilde
The Importance of Being Earnest

Tennessee Williams
A Streetcar Named Desire
The Glass Menagerie

Jeanette Winterson
Oranges Are Not the Only Fruit

John Webster
The Duchess of Malfi

Virginia Woolf
To the Lighthouse

William Wordsworth
The Prelude and Selected Poems

W.B. Yeats
Selected Poems

Metaphysical Poets